THE FUTURE OF MANKIND

THE
FUTURE
OF MANKIND

—————— Second Edition ——————

Tara Singh

Ballantine Books · New York

ACKNOWLEDGMENTS

I am grateful for the goodness of the following friends for their assistance in the preparation of this edition of *The Future of Mankind*:

Lucille Frappier, Charles Johnson, Howard and Bette Schneider, Frank Nader, and Norah Ryan.

I am most grateful to Cheryl Woodruff and Jim Cheatham for their contributions in editing this book.

CONTENTS

FOREWORD

I have discovered that fear and insecurity are not dissolved by fame and financial success. In fact, generally, money produces the fear of loss and anxiety to have more money.

The Future of Mankind is a book for those who have discovered the emptiness and non-fulfillment of materialism. It is a book for those who believe that fulfillment can be produced by more consumption and the pursuit of success. It is a book for people looking for fulfillment and peace.

Today, many are unaware that they live in a deep resignation that nothing they do will make a difference. In the midst of affluence, they live in a poverty of unfulfillment.

My service as a Commissioner on the U.S. Commission on Civil Rights has shown me that poverty is not merely the absence of money. Rather, I have seen that there are two kinds of poverty—one is insufficient money for food, clothing, and shelter. The other more grinding and despairing poverty is an absence of opportunity to sell your work in the marketplace and to be valued for the contribution you can make to another. The second kind of poverty allows for no dignity. In *The Future of Mankind*, Tara Singh presents his plan for ending both kinds of poverty.

This book shows a path that is different from the path we have come. It is a path that, when followed, can end poverty, separation, isolation and loneliness. It is a path that leads to stillness and peace. It is the still mind that has the clarity to see the world differently. It is the still mind that is not deceived or distracted by the artificial. And it is from the still and peaceful mind that we begin to experience gratitude and the ability to give.

Tara Singh's "Joseph Plan" and the spiritual practices that he teaches can renew our awareness of our connection to all mankind and reawaken us to the power of service. He invites us to discover a different path, as he quotes from *A Course in Miracles*, [1] saying:

> "When you come to the place where the branch in the road is quite apparent, you cannot go ahead. You must go one way or the other . . . The whole purpose of coming this far was to decide which branch you will take now. The way you came no longer matters. It can no longer serve. No one who reaches this far can make the wrong decision, although he can delay." [2]

Russell G. Redenbaugh
Commissioner, U.S. Commission on Civil Rights

TRANSFORMATION

It happens suddenly. There is a Voice
That speaks one Word, and everything is changed.

You understand an ancient parable
That seemed to be obscure. And yet it meant
Exactly what it said. The trivial
Enlarge in magnitude, while what seemed large
Resumes the littleness that is its due.
The dim grow bright, and what was bright before
Flickers and fades and finally is gone.
All things assume the role that was assigned
Before time was, in ancient harmony
That sings of Heaven in compelling tones
Which wipe away the doubting and the care
All other roles convey. For certainty
Must be of God.
                It happens suddenly,
And all things change. The rhythm of the world
Shifts into concert. What was harsh before
And seemed to speak of death now sings of life,
And joins the chorus to eternity.
Eyes that were blind begin to see, and ears
Long deaf to melody begin to hear.
Into the sudden stillness is reborn
The Ancient singing of creation's song,
Long silenced but remembered. By the tomb
The angel stands in shining hopefulness
To give salvation's message: "Be you free,
And stay not here. Go on to Galilee."*

*This poem is from *The Gifts of God* by Dr. Helen Schucman, the
Scribe of *A Course in Miracles* (Foundation for Inner Peace, 1982),
page 64. It is an incomparable book of poetry containing some of the
most important words ever spoken.

PART I

THE
STATUS QUO

Every decision you make
stems from what you think you are,
and represents the value
that you put upon yourself.

Believe the little can content you,
and by limiting yourself
you will not be satisfied.
For your function is not little,
and it is only by finding your function
and fulfilling it
that you can escape from littleness. [1]

The Future of Mankind

Eminent and renowned men and women have talked about non-violence and decentralization. They have warned us about the exploitation and catastrophe resulting from concentration of power in the hands of the few. They have pointed out that with the increase of industrialization and the commercialization of the media, the nations of the world would turn from being a means for the welfare of their people to an end in themselves. A few people have foreseen the consequences of artificial life and the irresponsibility of waste. They appealed to the masses; they had a cause.

Yet the great economists, statesmen, reformers, and scientists have not succeeded in harmonizing and humanizing society. The consequences of affluence and routine life are staring us in the face. The plague of unemployment is upon us, and those who have given their life energy to the artificial and the unessential are now self-spent, faced with their own irresponsibility. Human energy continues to be drained to build industrial economies that thrive on the manufacture of armament. Where is wisdom?

Never in the history of humanity have the instruments of death been so perfected, and so much time and energy allotted to destructive means. Never in history has the efficiency of tax collecting been so thoroughly mastered; nor has the manufacture of artificiality been so commercialized and wasted lives so adored. Never before has educated ignorance been so glorified. Never before has overpopulation gotten so out of hand.

Devoid of wisdom, what is the future of mankind? How few people have their own water to drink. Where is the self-sufficiency of the family or the self-reliance of the individual?

We may well be nearing unemployment of catastrophic proportions. [1] Anything could set it off—an energy crisis, one simple upheaval of earth changes. Even now the slightest economic imbalance can topple the job structure. The economy, monetary system, transportation —no area is truly self-sufficient.

In this complex interdependency, how quickly things could degenerate. Violence and inhumanity could patrol the land. Everyone's life is at stake against the tyranny of hunger, fear, and homelessness.

What will sustain us through the turmoil of the future if today's profit-oriented agricultural systems, electronics, and banking systems—with all their technology—break down? If the system collapses, what do you think it will resort to if not severe taxation? Conformity would become mandatory as a means of control. To cope with lawlessness and disorder, in our horror of scarcity, we would turn against the citizen the vicious means already invented to destroy our so-called enemies. Technology would turn into a god to which we would have to give our life and energy.

With the artificiality of modern life, lack of wisdom the world over has crowded people into cities that hardly produce anything that sustains life. Yet hunger and thirst are ever there, whether supermarkets are open or not. This, one of the most wasteful cultures ever known to history, could overnight be a victim of scarcity.

These are not prophecies or psychic predictions of doom, but realistic observations of industrial and governmental trends.

We thought education would help. Has it? Is man any less conformed? Education, for the most part, provides skills to suit unworthy jobs. Educated for jobs, we are drilled in skills to function in the monetary system of an abstract world. Look how powerfully this abstract culture influences the multitude. Who has a voice of his own or the simplicity of wisdom? Who lives by eternal values?

A sense of helplessness surrounds man today. He is ruled by insecurity and unfulfillment, pressured by time and problems. Man has already lost his own intrinsic work and is subject to a job; thus, he has become false to himself. He has lost the discrimination and wisdom to make his own decisions. He lives by mere choices.

This is the price we are paying for being slaves of gratification and pleasure which know no freedom, only dependence on another. Everywhere in the world it is the same. We have all but lost confidence in ourselves and in our own holiness. Jobs have become important and survival is what we worship. The present misuse of human energy is inconsistent with Higher Laws and will not work.

What God created, He protects. But man, enslaved by profiteering minds, controlled by political systems and corporate monopolies, has moved toward a mercenary civilization. Frustration's need for outlets, and in turn for money, is the universal epidemic. Like a seed, everything extends what it is.

Insecurity is not the issue. Productivity is the issue. True productivity eliminates insecurity. The paradox is that it is our jobs that maintain the insecurity. Today's productivity is linked with the irrelevant. It is the meaningless made essential.

Could you conceive of any culture in the history of mankind that was as concerned with money as we are today? Money is becoming as important as the water we drink and the air we breathe. Therefore, we are subject to someone else's control. Money is in charge and is the dictator of the age. It controls government agencies and most of mankind.

Because of money-making motives, it is not likely that powerful interests—the heads of corporations—will allow peace to exist. The industrial economy does not prosper with peace. It needs war to profit, and human life has become less important than the industrial economy. Henry David Thoreau said:

> "Peace of the world lies not in inventions but in
> men's hearts and men's souls . . . to sustain life,
> we need less rather than more; to protect life, we
> need courage and integrity, not weapons, not
> coalitions."

Everything is being taken over by the big industries—the dinosaurs of the modern age. The whole of humanity suffers, and the gain is only for the few. And this economy is worshipped everywhere!

This is where the meaningless routine of making a living has led us. When we have vested interest and greed, we get exploited. Can you see how decadence is coming into being?

I wish that we could see that the hysteria of self-centeredness and the incessant need to work is not necessary. Then we would learn to afford honesty and would get to know what is of internal value, irrespective of the externals.

How we have deceived ourselves! We seem incapable of being the witness to this movement of external society going toward its self-destruction in the name of progress. There was a time when the human being thought of himself as a human being. Now we are citizens. Citizens belong to some abstract idea or to wars for which they can kill another human being they have never seen before.

Where is humanism?
Where is love?
Where is reverence for Life?
Would the action of love extend hate, war, and prejudice?

In the early part of this century, Swami Vivekananda, a foremost disciple of Sri Ramakrishna, said:

"In the political struggle man must grow continually . . . He has duties toward his wife, his children, his parents. He has others toward his village, his town, his district, and finally, his country. But all these selfish interests for

which he strives so hard are transcended when
he becomes a citizen of humanity as a whole,
when he sees God Himself in each man he
serves. Such a man can move worlds, when his
tiny ego is dead and God has taken its
place." [2]

Anyone who speaks the truth must point out the insanity of our times and challenge the authority that con-
forms people. If he cares for you he must point it out to
wake you up and bring you to a state that is not deceived.

The issue is irresponsibility. We know conformity; we
know duty. We live in a culture where we are told what to
do by colleges, by parents, by jobs, by the media. We are
indoctrinated and conditioned. How dependent we are.
Our knowledge is mostly other people's knowings, nothing direct. These are the appalling discoveries we have to
make.

When you are responsible you know no conformity.
You are responsible for your life, for your ethics, for your
virtue.

A new action has to be born in America. We have to
see the detriment that progress has become, but not in
America alone. I am talking about what technology has
done to man all over the world: he is always pursuing the
advantage, always led by wishes. Can we see this, not as a
blame but as a fact in itself so that we can come to urgency? Then we are stepping out of the fascination with
the external that blossomed here and we turn the tide. We
become part of the vibration of the land, of the New
World, and we begin to outgrow the externals.

We have to see that century after century everything we have done in the name of progress, in the name of science, in the name of religion, in the name of education, has made us more and more conscious of self-survival. And now we are at the mercy of the system.

See how universally destructive progress has become and be determined not to be a part of it. We must change. Instead of feeling helpless we must find our own potential and relate with other forces rather than with nationalism or man-made laws. The responsibility is ours.

We are who we are because we have limited ourselves to a very small sphere of existence, with its greed and fear, wishing and wanting. Yet life is more than self-survival.

Wherever there is attachment or vested interest we become threatened. And the person we like the least is the one who brings the gift of truth. Such men have rotted in prison, been assassinated, and crucified.

It does not matter where we are in the world, the principle is the same: beyond "me and mine" it is difficult for us to go. We are in the bondage of our beliefs. If what you believe is different from what I believe, then there is inevitably a clash.

Can we come to some kind of receptivity knowing that reaction is caused by what we believe? This is where mankind is limited today, as he has been throughout the ages.

More money is spent on armament today than at any time in the whole history of mankind. Countries that cannot afford the luxury of toilet paper maintain armies and sophisticated, deadly weapons. Ours is no longer a war against the capitalist or the socialist; it is a war against the human being.

Wake up!

YOU are the human being!

And you support this tragedy with your prejudices.

Carl Sandburg said there is only one man in the world and his name is All Men. Fear has no nationality. Greed, hunger, sex, have no nationality. All men have the same brain. Thinking itself, said Mr. J. Krishnamurti, is common to all men in spite of poverty, illiteracy, sophistication, or affluence. We all think with the same brain.

The technology of computers and mass communications has now advanced to the point of shaping man's very brain and controlling his thinking—almost completely to the advantage of those in control of the system. The horror of this grim fact already at work is perhaps the worst nightmare mankind has ever known. Yet the perversity is hardly visible and we are in danger of being reduced to mere robots. Science now attempts to affect the human species.

Through the control of educational institutions, religious belief systems, political propaganda, and the financial supremacy of vested interests, we are being molded to a sub-human level to function as programmed. As the human brain is being fully manipulated hardly anyone will be able to cope with the ingenious methods of external influence. Man himself, for the first time, is at stake now that the nuclear age with its ultra-modern electronic technology is upon the planet.

With industry's frantic search for consumer markets and the push for military supremacy, the tension among nations mounts to explosive points. Violence, greed, and might roam the earth like giant monsters in the guise of corporations and big business. Meanwhile, the New Age commercial "gurus" sell their positive platitudes and cosmic transformations. Man, already in the delirium of nationalism, is not fully aware of what is ahead for the mechanized society.

As violence, distrust, decadence, panic, and the craze for armament increase, life on the planet is affected. Where each person is limited to his own vested interest, the outcome of flourishing self-centeredness will surely lead to consequences.

In Third World countries, the population explosion is most rampant and least controlled because there is not much they can do. Even if their gross national revenue were spent on population control—at the cost or neglect of agricultural projects and other necessities of life—it would not be in proportion to the problem. Sufficient resources at the national level are not available.

It is a human problem, however, not a national one. The resources at the human level are adequate, though mankind lacks the humanism to employ them. The problems that remain unresolved result in devastating consequences.

Politics and religion, which are beginning to compete for supremacy, are also becoming dependent on the invisible bosses who are in control of the monetary system of the world. The cost of elections is so high that in most cases the candidates have become subject to the control of those in charge—for the simple reason that for them to come to prominence requires big money.

Behold the profile of our times!

The question is, can humanity be helped externally? Society is not apt to change; but it is still possible for the individual to come to an inner transformation. The only possible transformation is change within the individual. To settle for personal survival or advantage is not sufficient.

Where, then, is the gratefulness that inspires man and brings him to the action of the soul—the indefatigable spirit of creation? Do you not see that man is tired without the energy of love and his contact with God? Would you not like to be free from the preoccupation of fear and insecurity, and the torment of conflict within and without?

As long as man has lived he has tried to avoid wars and thereby maintained them. If our interest is truly in avoiding war we will end the conflict in ourselves, for that is where it springs from. External war merely manifests what is there in each person. As long as we have reactions, likes, and dislikes, there will be war. It is as simple as that.

So, how do we end war? We end it within ourselves. Coming to peace within is the ending of war.

> "The true glory is reserved not for the man who can throw a bomb, but for him who can stand up and say, 'I possess nothing but God.'"[3]

Our basic problem is that we do not heed what the wise have to say. It is all there. And obvious too. But we remain caught in the misperceptions of our own knowing and irresponsibility remains the statement of our lives.

We have to reverse our dependence on the externals so as not to rely solely on the body senses. This is the step we have to take. And yet so few have taken a step beyond the physical senses. Joy is in the humility of a modest life not driven by unfulfillment.

Contemporary man has such little knowing of Divine Laws, hardly any relationship with truth and peace of mind, or contact with his own inner resources. His vast potentials remain unexplored. How few the world over are the men who are not ruled by the external, who love one another, and who yearn for the sanity of righteousness.

The wise person sees that "me and mine" has no existence in reality. He sees the deception of ideas, that they are abstract; the illusion of the future, that it is self-projected. He sees the fallacy of accomplishment, that it projects future fears and violates the purity of trust in the spirit.

We are so afraid to trust in virtue and to see the good in a brother. Love and thoughtfulness are related to Heaven, to laws that govern the universe. When man has learned to give, he is in charge of the very planetary system.

To know the truth of Love and to extend it is the challenge each individual has to face. It is not the changing of an opinion or a concept; it requires an internal correction. Trapped in the illusions of his own physical senses, mankind as a whole has avoided this action throughout the centuries.

The virtuous action of "LOVE YE ONE ANOTHER" will survive the failure of economy or any other disaster. For when we start with giving we are productive out of the abundance of a just life. The action of our care for the brother is complete unto itself. To Grace, external scarcity is not a fact. We need to be a strength to another and this is achieved by the mastery of life within.

We have the resources and the capacity to change. No matter what our individual situations are, all that is required is our pure intent. No one need be pressured into helplessness. Change is an internal action that starts with self.

Therefore, will you resort to the expedience of the system or will you live according to your own conviction?

Out of this chaotic environment and the insanity of our times, with its tremendous capacity to abuse human energy and the energy of nature, is given the self-reliant action of *A Course in Miracles*. It helps us discover that survival is not the goal of life, salvation is. Man has searched and yearned for lifetimes for the keys inherent in *A Course in Miracles*; saints and prophets have tried to give us a glimpse of the glory and splendor of a thought-free state. Now the *Course* has come with its step-by-step curriculum and, with it, the light to awaken us to awareness.

A Course in Miracles states most encouragingly:

"In my defenselessness my safety lies."

*You who feel threatened by this changing world,
its twists of fortune and its bitter jests, its brief*

relationships and all the "gifts" it merely lends to take away again; attend this lesson well. The world provides no safety. It is rooted in attack, and all its "gifts" of seeming safety are illusory deceptions. It attacks, and then attacks again. No peace of mind is possible where danger threatens thus.

The world gives rise but to defensiveness. For threat brings anger, anger makes attack seem reasonable, honestly provoked, and righteous in the name of self-defense. . . .

Defenselessness is strength. It testifies to recognition of the Christ in you. Perhaps you will recall . . . that choice is always made between Christ's strength and your own weakness, seen apart from Him. Defenselessness can never be attacked, because it recognizes strength so great attack is folly. . . . And in defenselessness we stand secure, serenely certain of our safety. . . . For you will know that Heaven goes with you. [4]

Man is of divine origin. When we undermine that, we undervalue the action of Life itself.

When man is transformed,
the world is affected.

He is
the whole,
the totality of the universe.

2

Coming Events Cast
Their Shadow

Whenever a nation stands aloof from virtue and ethics, it becomes beguiled by the world of the senses. To the extent materialism succeeds, man becomes inwardly weak; and this is happening all over the world today. A preoccupation with buying, selling, loss, and gain prevails in the absence of love and goodness. It is a fraud against humanity. What influence will today's controlled multitude have on the new generation? Wisdom is required to turn the tide.

Humanism demands a change. That is the New World's destiny: to awaken itself and revolutionize the world. Humanism then flowers into self-reliance, having something of one's own to give, and finally, into service. But in this age of dependence on jobs how can one know and honor humanism? How can an accelerated society heed the call to the wisdom of its forefathers, "In God We Trust"?

Because America was the undisputed leader after World War II, whatever example it set would determine the trend for the rest of the planet. If the United States had cooperated with goodness and rightness, she could have lifted up the whole planet. This opportunity never existed before.

America could have caused a change. If she had she would have recognized and cooperated with leaders who had different values and ethics—the noble and wise—in other parts of the world. The premise of our foreign policy would have been very different. We could have produced a world free of war, rather than one of political power blocs.

America's industrial affluence was an experiment for the world. Why did it not set a new, humanistic course, but compel the world to militarize?

Gradually, a small minority began to monopolize political, military and industrial interests. They exaggerated the fear of communism and invented the Cold War. But perhaps most damaging, this small anti-democratic group which perpetrated a fraud upon the American people also became the enemies of wisdom throughout the world. Consistently, the wise, objective voices of other nations were ignored. Even today the independent voices of America itself are not fully heeded. There are consequences when a nation does not listen to those who have outgrown nationalism and society.

Today the planet has become divided in the interests of man-made dogmas seeking control over the minds of men, women, and children. A concentration of power in the hands of the few not only misleads but imposes a limitation upon its people.

When America wanted military bases in Egypt, ostensibly to counter the Soviet Union, Egyptian President Nasser said that his country feared "these defense pacts are a new sort of colonialism." He noted that Britain and France had dominated the Middle East for a long time while Russia had never had any influence there.

President Nasser added that at the end of World War II, "the Middle East was looking to America as the saviour, the new country that was rising to liberate us from domination. We were looking to America with faith." But within a decade Nasser was disillusioned, seeing that "you [America] supported the colonial countries against the countries who want to be free."

One wonders what the facts actually were, and who decided that Russia was a threat in the Middle East? The media usually prints what government officials say, and soon most people are thinking similarly. Even Thomas Jefferson said, however,

> "The man who never looks into a newspaper is better informed than he who reads them, inasmuch as he who knows nothing is nearer the truth than he whose mind is filled with falsehoods and errors."

Strong nations seek to exact global influence either through colonial occupation, the establishment of military bases, or various forms of economic and political intervention. It is this involvement in the affairs of others, as well as the exercise of force needed to maintain this position, which produces consequences. After the Second World War America could have turned the tide to value humanism and goodness over its own military, economic, or political interests. But this challenge demanded wisdom.

America often violated its democratic principles and got involved in the affairs of other countries. Howard Zinn, in his book, *A People's History of the United States*, writes:

"By the end of the Vietnam War, 7 million tons of bombs had been dropped on Vietnam, more than twice the total bombs dropped in Europe and Asia in World War II—almost one 500-pound bomb for every human being in Vietnam. In addition, poisonous sprays were dropped by planes to destroy trees and any kind of growth—an area the size of the state of Massachusetts was covered with such poison."

Millions of Vietnamese lost their lives, 58,000 Americans were killed and 365,000 Americans were wounded in the war. The money spent totalled over $172 billion. How great was the cost of the Vietnam War in terms of human life? How great was the profit made by the military-industrial complex? It was an utterly unessential war, but surely profitable to the arms manufacturers and other industries.

And yet there were wise voices who offered warning, including Indian Prime Minister Indira Gandhi. Buckminster Fuller, speaking of her in an inscription, wrote:

"To Indira, in whose integrity God is entrusting much of the evolutionary success of humanity and with utter safety."[1]

Shortly before her assassination at the hands of her bodyguards, she herself wrote:

"If I die a violent death as some fear and a few are plotting, I know the violence will be in the thought and the action of the assassin, not in my dying. . . ."[2]

She warned the U.S. regarding the escalation of war in Indochina, urging us that war should be against poverty not against communism.

French President Charles de Gaulle had withdrawn from Vietnam to focus on his own country's needs. In June, 1961, at a meeting in Paris with President John Kennedy, he said:

> "You will find that intervention in this area will be an endless entanglement. Once a nation has been aroused, no foreign power, however strong, can impose its will upon it. You will discover this for yourselves. For even if you find local leaders who in their own interests are prepared to obey you, the people will not agree to it, and indeed do not want you. The ideology you invoke will make no difference. Indeed, in the eyes of the masses it will become identified with your will to power. That is why the more you become involved out there against Communism, the more the Communists will appear as the champions of national independence, and the more support they will receive, if only from despair. . . . I predict that you will sink step by step into a bottomless military and political quagmire, however much you spend in men and money. What you, we and others ought to do for unhappy Asia is not to take over the running of these States ourselves, but to provide them with the means to escape from the misery and humiliation which, there as elsewhere, are the causes of totalitarian regimes. I tell you this in the name of the West." [3]

Former Indian Prime Minister Jawaharlal Nehru was a statesman whom President John Kennedy had compared to Abraham Lincoln. One need only read his account, *Glimpses of World History*, to make contact with his enormous scope of mind. His was a voice of sanity in an unstable world. Former United Nations Secretary General U Thant said of Jawaharlal Nehru:

> "He was not only a great man, but a good man. His extraordinary qualities endeared him not only to the people of India but to people all over the world who had at heart peace, justice and equality for mankind."[4]

French President Charles de Gaulle said of Pandit Nehru:

> "This great man, for whom the cause of humanity was inseparable from the cause of the Indian people, his plans continually disappointed by the magnitude of the task, but unshakable in his faith and unwearying in his efforts, outlined to me the gigantic problems of subsistence and unity with which his country was faced, and the ways in which mine might help to alleviate them, not without ultimate benefit to herself."[5]

Prime Minister Nehru, in a United Nations speech, spoke about:

> ". . . a world without war—a world based on the cooperation of nations and peoples. It is not merely a world where war is kept in check, or a balancing of armed forces. It is much deeper than that. It is a world from which the major

causes of war have been removed, and social structures built up which further peaceful cooperation, within a nation, as well as between nations."

America presently enjoys an external security built on fear. Yet we must realize that true security lies in rightness. Can America afford peace now? Will industrialization allow it? There are times when one wonders who owns the government.

On June 7, 1981, then Speaker of the House of Representatives, Mr. Thomas (Tip) O'Neill, appeared on ABC's *Issues and Answers*. He said that America's political system was being controlled by the "selfish"—the wealthy, upper echelon of the nation. He warned that the middle American who built the country upon certain principles and ideals was being forgotten and could one day wake up to find that America had been destroyed.

A wise head of state does not resort to expedience and compromise. Having reverence for Life, he has recognized the inflexible law of cause and effect which regulates external forces and has dire consequences.

One who will not contradict the Will of God discovers that non-cooperation and economic sanctions will work to resolve international disputes and lead mankind to a war-free world. When kindness and friendship with another nation fails to end disagreement, the wisdom of non-violence and non-cooperation will succeed if moral strength accompanies them.

On August 2, 1990, Iraqi soldiers invaded Kuwait. The United Nations called for the imposition of economic sanctions on Iraq. The exclusive use of sanctions could have ushered in an age in which war was abolished. On January 17, 1991, however, a military force dominated by America launched a full-scale bombing campaign against Iraq. Of the 2,000 combat aircraft flown, approximately 1,800 were American.

The loss of sanctions as a means of peaceful resolution is a tragedy. It may have required years for the goals of the sanctions to be accomplished, but they could have been made to work for humanity's sake if the intent was one of peace. To end war is a just and noble aspiration in man. The harmony between America and the Soviet Union offered the opportunity to direct money and skills toward honoring the sacredness of life on the planet.

Instead, the resulting war with Iraq publicized American industry's modern weapons, and at the same time displayed the ineffectiveness of other nation's military hardware, now rendered virtually obsolete.

America's preparation for war in the Persian Gulf had actually begun years before. According to government figures, from 1982 through 1989 the U.S. alone sold $24.5 billion worth of military equipment to Saudi Arabia.

An essay by Strobe Talbott in the January 13, 1992, *Time Magazine* reported:

> "In November 1990, during the buildup to Operation Desert Storm, James Baker tried to shore up support on the home front for the dispatch of U.S. troops half a world away. 'To bring it down to the level of the average American citizen,' he said, 'standing up to Saddam

Hussein *means jobs*.' Then, to make sure everyone understood, he did it again. 'If you want to sum it up in one word, it's *jobs*.' "

Is it true that America has come to the point where wars have become a political and commercial necessity? Only kindness and compassion can succeed in humanizing society. The question is, "Can America afford a world free of war?"

"Might is right" may appeal to the profiteering segment of society, but it inevitably results in disaster—first abroad and then at home. The awesome national debt will compel the government to resort to unthinkable justifications. Irresponsibility and our perfected military machine could lead prosperous America to lean and hungry days at home.

Sadly, even before reaching maturity the United States began to decline. Within a decade America has become the largest debtor nation in the world. Its immense national debt will be a liability for generations to come. The cost of paying interest on the current debt of $3.7 trillion will be approximately $23.5 million per hour in 1992. [6]

The following is an excerpt from economist, diplomat, and author John Kenneth Galbraith's editorial on "The Price of Comfort" which appeared in newspapers across the country on January 6, 1991.

"In the United States, the price of past error has reached truly formidable proportions and with, alas, consequences going far beyond our frontiers. There has been much discussion in these last years of the increasing interdependence of

nations—the global economy. One consequence is that all must suffer for the actions and
errors of any one government and people, and
especially if they are those of a country as large
and important on the world scene as the United
States.

"The American prospect, as we enter the second
year of the new decade and end 10 years of
free-enterprise rediscovery in Washington, is far
from bright. And from the United States the
shadow of financial instability, economic reces-
sion, unemployment and uncertain government
extends out to the world."

Despite enormous debt and rising unemployment, the
five days of presidential inaugural festivities in 1989 cost
$30 million, making it the most expensive inauguration in
America's history.

When a country is rich and in control, it is a law—like
the lion in the jungle. But the little cubs also grow and
eventually take the old lion's place. There may well be
violence as America weakens. Not having given importance to moral strength within, America will continue to
rely on the external. It may result in a police state, for
nothing is going to be safe. People will be subjected to
more and more conformity and control. The situation
could be conducive to a military takeover. The externals
are in control when man lacks moral values. It is as if
people are drugged by outlets and pacified with indulgences.

Nothing the world has ever faced will resemble what
will happen in America, since we have violated right rela-

tionship with the land, sea, and sky. Nature too may revolt. Deterioration is flourishing and the world is caught in the horrible grip of consequences.

As America declines, what will happen in the rest of the world? Two expansionary nations achieved prominence after World War II—Israel and China. Right now America supports them both. But the future belongs to China.

China has become strong because in its isolation—imposed by the West for decades—it had to come to self-sufficiency. Indian Prime Minister Indira Gandhi said,

> "Perhaps if China had not been so isolated it wouldn't have been so aggressive. It would have been more possible to bring it within a certain discipline."[7]

For years, as an act of intimidation, America paraded its Seventh Fleet up and down the waters of China's coast. America also acknowledged the tiny island of Formosa as the real China and effectively campaigned to keep mainland China out of the United Nations. That was the case until U.S. business interests determined that in order to obtain a new marketplace, mainland China would have to be recognized. Overnight the "red" in Red China disappeared without a trace.

Destiny and the West's consequences combine to pass leadership to another people. Today the Arabs are divided and lack leadership. But China will ally with the Asian nations and give them the strength they have longed for. Central Asia's Moslems—whose energies and capacities are more advanced than those of some of the desert dwellers—will join with China and the Arab world to challenge the declining West. The two factors—expansion and alliance—may very well make it possible for China to extend all the way to the Mediterranean. China has a destiny. All the yellow races are rising as though preordained.

Japan, too, through the efficiency of manufacturing is compelling the U.S. automobile industry to falter in its attempt to survive. Other industries will follow. America could never have imagined that her international dominance of the aerospace industry would be threatened by Japan but it is only a matter of time before Japan will surpass her in the manufacturing of commercial aircraft.

America's last chance was to ally with Russia. But we did not support the wise statesman, Mikhail Gorbachev, who oversaw the bloodless dismantling of an empire. One wonders whether capitalism could end without bloodshed. Russia walked out of country after country it had controlled, and divided up its own political union. Will America be as farsighted when Alaska and Hawaii want to be independent of the United States?

We did not recognize Mikhail Gorbachev's unique voice, nor appreciate his nobility. One is baffled that such wisdom was accessible to mankind. How few were aware of it. America now gives preferred trading status to China which massacred its dissident students in Tiananmen Square. In doing so America is cooperating with its future rival, and has opposed the Russians who need friendship and help. Hardly anyone pays much heed to the widespread inconsistencies. What causes this indifference?

Mikhail Gorbachev stayed consistent with his principles as he gave freedom to Eastern Europe. People were allowed to choose their governments even though Gorbachev knew they might go against him. Most politicians would not have been able to give up that power without violence. As with other great beings throughout history, his seeming failure was his greatest success. Mikhail Gorbachev's loss of political power, and the subsequent ending of the Soviet Union, represents the world's inability to embrace his uncompromising wisdom.

Around this time Poland and other newly-democratic countries appealed to the U.S. for economic aid. But what they were given was not in proportion to their human needs. One cannot help but question how much more help Poland would have received if it had been in an armed struggle with communist Russia.

Military aid is the focal point of America's foreign policy. So much U.S. money has been poured into the Philippines and Pakistan that one would think they should be industrial giants by now. But the assistance is largely in the form of military hardware to these non-democratic nations. From 1954 to 1963, America spent over $1 billion supplying and training Pakistan's armed forces.

Who provided the funds, and who realizes the benefits? Do living standards for Filipinos and Pakistanis improve as a result of military assistance? Does trade with U.S. companies increase? Does goodwill rise between the nations? Recently Imelda Marcos, widow of the former ruler of the Philippines, was arrested in Manila. She was accused of stealing as much as $5 billion during the twenty-year Marcos dictatorship, much of which was paid by American taxpayers. Yet, she and her husband, Ferdinand Marcos, were welcomed and honored as guests of the American people. Where the "laws of justice have become subject to the laws of injustice,"[8] the consequences are that we have little that is vertical to impart to the next generation. How can we expect our children to listen to our words which are devoid of truth and thoughtfulness?

America's downfall began with abuse of human potential and the misuse of industrial might. Its industries sought profit in promoting a life of artificiality, not in meeting the primary needs of man on which survival rests.

What we are describing here may seem negative, but one needs to see what is ahead. America's lifestyle of outlets, indulgences, and distractions may well come to an end. The discovery of inner resources has not been a national priority. Instead, we have externalized our lives to a dangerous degree. There is inherent disorder in over-externalization and frustration.

Will economic chaos wake up the American people? Perhaps mass unemployment and the challenge to easy and comfortable lives will bring about a change of values.

To make internal correction is probably the least enticing path to take. We face, at every turn, external opposition from society's vested interests by which we are virtually controlled, as well as all our own fears and misperceptions. However, the will to exchange fear for love is always there. We need to make contact with our everlasting holiness and peace, gather our own strength, and not be affected by the externals.

Our pressured lives today hardly allow the entry of awareness. There is just the compelling urge to join the collective, to revel in "the highest standard of living in the world." Such pressure dampens the sanity of stillness and forbids a life of serenity. It rules us, and does not even give the space to question the momentum of a world where half-truths have become an expedience.

Only wisdom and humanism are free of conflict and consequences. Humanism has no outer activity. But we are drawn to activities, which then pressure us. And a pressured person likes affluence, because it provides outlets and indulgences. Pleasure's stimulation makes us dependent on pleasure itself, whereas serenity, having its own inner potentials, is ever free.

Emerson said,

"There are people who have an appetite for grief, pleasure is not strong enough. . . ."

For decades, America has wallowed in the world of pleasure even while it was inflicting the pain of war upon weaker nations halfway around the world. The era of pleasure is coming to an end, and grief is staring us in the face. How will the mercenary civilization tied to jobs deal with it when there is not the strength of rightness in their lives?

Mother Teresa said,

"There are people in America that are so lonely they wish they could die."

There is an urgent need in America to take care of those living in the slums, the tens of thousands of people in the large cities that are compelled to live at a sublevel of existence. According to the *Children's Defense Fund* every

35 seconds an infant is born into poverty in the United States and every 14 minutes an American infant dies in the first year of life.

During the six weeks the U.S. was fighting in the Persian Gulf, according to the *National Association of Religious Women*, 1,250 U.S. infants and children died from poverty, 4,000 died due to low birth weight, and 1,825 were killed or injured by guns. Is not the human being more important than building a war machine or spending hundreds of billions of dollars on space exploration?

The New World is a land of abundance in a world haunted by famine. Wars in the future could be fought over food supplies. Now life gives humanity a space in which to change. We have a decade to correct our outlook.

A change of presidents is not going to make much difference because the President represents and is part of mass consciousness. The political situation is such that most of the same Congressmen and Senators return to Washington after each election. Mere enthusiasm will not correct the approach to life that has become the genetic pattern of America. Any real correction can take place after the lean years; the true spirit of America will rise. Whoever undermines the Divine Emanation of man sees only blood and bones. The New World will come to its own expression for the first time.

In the end, neither materiality nor poverty is the issue. Man's separation from wholeness is the issue. Within wholeness everything extends what it is, and there is a sharing of love that intensifies the Source of Creation. Without the light of the heart our lives are meaningless; without the love of honesty it is not possible to make contact with the sacredness within. It is gratefulness that introduces man to humanism.

Humanism and the reversal process could begin in America. The underdeveloped Third World is too enamored by indulgent Western lifestyles to consider changing. But in America, disillusionment and transformation are possible. America is energetic. It need not go toward violence. America could become the first nation to realize that affluence without wisdom is self-destructive. It could totally change the vibration of the planet.

Now that America is the only superpower, non-violence is possible. War can be abolished and the New World's destiny of bringing peace and prosperity to all mankind can be fulfilled. America can restore credibility to the use of economic sanctions rather than destructive force in the resolution of international disputes. Through arms control, it could also prevent other ambitious nations from becoming superpowers.

America has to change its own relationship to the United Nations and allow the U.N. to honor its original intent, so that poorer nations are helped rather than manipulated in the interest of political power blocs. We have to rise to a non-nationalistic perspective.

The population explosion of the Third World has gotten out of control, and resources at the level of nationalism cannot deal with it. It is a problem that can be solved only at the human level, for the resources are there. Goodwill in America is enough to awaken mankind to a new age by putting energy into solving the problems of over-population. Similarly, it can meet the primary needs of mankind everywhere.

In 1948, America initiated the Point Four Program, known as the Marshall Plan. It said, "The only war we seek is the war against poverty, disease, illiteracy, and hunger." Later, however, it became subject to political intrigue. It is now time for us to recognize that only humanism is consistent with meeting the primary needs of man for food, shelter, and clothing. This must be kept free from politics and preferences.

We have the technology to help all nations meet their needs and move toward self-sufficiency. It could become a joyous joint venture where profit is not the motive. In doing so America would benefit along with the rest of humanity. Shifting attention and production toward sanity would solve the problem of unemployment. Only by feeding the hungry of the world will we be able to feed our own people, subject as they are to jobs.

The goodness and right use of science, technology, and industry would enliven America and honor the spirit of "In God We Trust." In the end, "In God We Trust" could become a benediction to all mankind. Goodness cannot fail. The American people would respond to it. Turning to rightness demands conviction, but there is no risk in it. Herein lies salvation for this country.

Never has a single nation had the resources and opportunity to implement such thoughtfulness. The purity of the intent that would do so is not external to Divine Laws. Its scope is vast. For its virtue and goodness, all Universal Forces would stand behind it. We would no longer be working against the laws of creation, but replenishing the planet and protecting all that lives upon it.

3

Goodness Will Bring Peace to the Earth

Intimation is like a seed. Everything that is created comes from the Thought of God, and then manifests into matter. A seed is as powerful as the Thought Itself, and therefore goes on. Not subject to time, it unfolds in its own way and extends what it is for millions of years.

As more jobs are lost and unemployment looms like a gigantic monster, political systems are challenged. Politics all over the world now suffers from its own insecurity and falseness. Out of frustration, greed, and the desire for power, it disguises itself and resorts to war—which is quite profitable for some. Governments everywhere are spiritually barren, and national affairs are degenerating into crisis. Transformation—so sorely needed—cannot occur when there is personal motive.

Politicians in most countries have become the enemies of their own people. They have no need to turn to virtuous values because compromises succeed without disturbing anyone. In a world of interpretation, everything can be justified, especially by the present media. Educated mindlessness is in charge via expedience and pretense. Is not our society becoming more and more regulated by fear, insecurity, and scarcity?

Disaster runs ahead of all solutions. Unemployment in America will be accompanied by a moral degeneration never heard of on such a large scale. Yet it need not be. The God-created world has enough resources for everyone.

Is it not we who impose limitations on a glorious world of abundance? What is lacking is discrimination between the God-created and the man-made—the Real and the unreal. The Real is Absolute; the unreal is man's projection.

To be consistent with the Will of God is religious. "In God We Trust." If this were so, this nation would know no unfulfillment. As an idea it has no meaning. To transcend the intellect is to know the sacredness and power of one's own will, which is not subject to fear. But we have built everything on a false premise. Why do we have resistance to unity and harmony?

The will has no traits of personality. It never wants nor seeks to achieve since it knows no unfulfillment. In reality, the will undoes misperceptions and distortion. It is a cleanser of illusions. Intensified attention is awareness, the all-powerful will of man, one with God. Awareness has no activity in it. It is free of conflict and introduces man to his true, impersonal nature. Resistance and unwillingness to change are the issues. We want somehow to identify with our little self, remain preoccupied with "me and mine," and learn about self-improvement. Therefore, we depend on someone else telling us what to do.

Is this preoccupation not the very denial of one's own sacredness? God's Will and man's will are one. What men and nations lack is compassion. The very realization of this truth could effortlessly turn the tide. How little we

know of the power and purity of spontaneity that originates out of an unpressured moment of stillness in the
mind of man. Stop a moment. See how detrimental most
of man's external learning is now proving itself to be.

In true sharing one rises above sensation to the stillness of one's own being. Love knows the truth of service,
for it extends the very Source of Life Itself. Everything else
is of the relative level—this versus that. "LOVE YE ONE
ANOTHER" intensifies love, when shared among human
beings. Love is timeless and relates the human being to the
vision of Reality behind appearance. There is no light in
man's belief systems—be they political, economic, or religious—whereas the simplicity of a saint extends the kingdom of God on earth. He knows that nothing belongs to
us—neither the earth, the tree, nor the water—and yet it
is there to sustain life. We too, knowing this, would have
reverence and contentment in our relationship with the
universe. Having something to give we would be truly
productive. Fulfillment does not seek and our lives would
be a joy upon the earth. The presence of a holy person is
a blessing.

Unemployment can be dealt with if we rise to meet the
challenge. Humanism, having no lack, has the potentials.
We need a shift of energy and interest within the nation—
from vested interests to goodness. Man's compassion has
infinite resources. Our thoughtfulness to extend goodwill
to the "have nots" of the world would invoke Divine
Forces to support us in freeing humanity from hunger.
The change of objective is what is needed. Neither hunger
nor unemployment are problems in reality. They only
become problems when we lack goodness.

Man, in his goodness, is godlike. Peace and sanity will
awaken him to the joy of his own impeccable Self. Obvi-

ously the insanity of fear opposes the Law of Love. Our justice, championing punishment, violates justice itself. The Divine function of the human being is to extend Absolute Laws at the level of time and illusion. Only the wise, having overcome reaction and outgrown man-made, immature rules and concepts, can recognize the power of "turning the other cheek."

> *As forgiveness allows love to return to my awareness, I will see a world of peace and safety and joy.* [1]

What would remove wrong-mindedness in societies and nations? It would have to be a sense of responsibility in the individual willing to make internal corrections at the level of misperception. His own attention awakens potentials within and the power of his own will undoes self-deception. The awareness of his own sacredness introduces him to holy relationship, forever observant but free of judgment, with every living being. The ending of conflict within a small number of earnest people can transform the world.

Behold the insanity of our overly externalized world and its direction by which the individual is seduced and compelled to conform. Under the leadership of America since World War II, the military budget of most nations has skyrocketed, even in countries which hardly have enough food to eat. As long as war is profitable, how can there be peace in the world?

We have trillions of dollars for the destruction of mankind and nature but little money for food for the poorer nations. No wonder the country is under debt, inviting hunger to its own back door. These are the consequences of patronizing violence, dividing humanity, and extending lovelessness.

What could prevent America from destroying itself? Where would you start? What would you do with vested interests that do not want change, having worked all things in their own favor? Neither nationalism, nor the present economic system, nor those currently in power, foster change. At what point in loss of integrity does it become impossible for a nation to renew itself?

Nationalism is not a law; it is a lingering tribal idea of man. When the human being and his nations violate Eternal Laws, then there is unemployment, war, or earthquakes. We have polluted the atmosphere so much that we are close to seeing a shifting of the poles and vast earth changes around the globe.

The fanfare of affluence did not heighten human consciousness. Everything that we can do without spiritual awareness we have tried, and it does not work. We cannot ignore that we are of the spirit without having consequences. At present, any solution that refers to the loftiness and sacredness of the spirit is pronounced impractical; whatever keeps mankind wallowing in sensation is promoted. But there is no need for America to hit the bottom. Seen as a warning, unemployment could be a good thing. True prosperity comes not from our labors, but from right relationship with the earth.

With the advent of American supremacy, mankind entered an age of tremendous scientific development. America could still lead the world by directing her technology to the primary needs of humanity—food, shelter, clothing. This country could produce enough to feed the nations of the Third World.

First provide food for the people in these under-developed countries, and then help them revolutionize their own agricultural development. This would transform their economies, increase their ability to produce, and benefit America's agriculture and economy too.

The age of using bullock carts and wooden plows pulled by oxen is over. Having thousands of water pumps would make the land more productive. The Food and Agriculture Organization (FAO) of the United Nations is fully familiar with what to do. It just needs to be supported. Could America come forth to do so? The know-how is there, but the help so far has not been in proportion to the need. There have been a lot of kind gestures—but now it has to be done on a vast scale. We have been trying to irrigate a field with a bucket of water.

In the early stages America could help get small projects in rural areas off the ground. It would require introducing the underdeveloped area to the industrial approach of mechanized farming. It is like lending a helping hand—starting with decentralized projects in remote areas so that they spread out and are not monopolized.

Each country could support its projects to its own capacity to begin with and pay for the equipment America provides at cost out of their new wealth. While there would be no profit in it, there would be no financial loss, either. The helper—America—could pay the salaries of its workers out of goodwill. Soldiers and sailors are already on salary, and could give themselves to service rather than to unemployment. They are well-organized and disciplined already, are used to doing what needs to be done, and know the resources of today's technology.

Once land is made productive and the primary needs of these nations are met, they would have the means to finance their own industries. This shift from aid to trade would help both America and the people who were once poor. The result would be a productive, ongoing relationship beneficial to the whole human race and a solution to unemployment at home.

Aid represents emergency measures and no country can rely upon it for long. The shift from aid to trade is miraculous. In trade, both nations prosper because the poorer nation can afford to buy equipment to industrialize its own country. Humanism works; replacing greed with goodness has more benefits than we realize.

After the Second World War, the population exploded. To a great extent prosperity itself would deal with the issue of population growth. This has already been demonstrated in Western societies.

A prosperous nation is responsible for extending harmonious goodwill. It is this thoughtfulness that gladdens the heart and leads to right relationship. Meeting the primary needs of man will energize this age. There is no reason why everyone in the world cannot be sheltered—owning his own home, even with a plot of land.

What is God's belongs to everyone,
and is his due. [2]

The challenge is to decentralize power, population, and wealth. Mere understanding is not good enough; it is a substitute for the Eternal Law.

> *The teachers of God have trust in the world, because they have learned it is not governed by the laws the world made up. It is governed by a Power That is in them but not of them. It is this Power That keeps all things safe.* [3]

What is real is real forever. It does not change, for Reality is part of Universal Laws. There is the Divine Hand in what is timeless that nothing external can affect. To goodness nothing is external, for it is Absolute.

Cruelty, problems, and deprivation arise as we move from right relationship to expedience. It is this that needs correction. The silent power of goodness brings prosperity to mankind. It can change climates and bring rain to a barren world. It is compassion that is lacking, not food.

> *All the help you can accept will be provided, and not one need you have will not be met.* [4]

Universal forces accompany the movement toward unity and harmony. Each race has its own intrinsic temperament, expression, and resources. Each region should be allowed the space to prosper and to flower in its own environment.

All resources are at the level of humanism. All resources are at the level of Life.

When we are related to the Source of Life, we are part of its abundance. Nationalism and other abstract concepts

and dogmas divide man and are largely the cause of insecurity and poverty in the world. But in Life there is no
lack. In right thinking there is no lack. Everything in
nature gives, whether it is fragrance or food. Rivers flow.
The sun shines. There is the silent purity of dew. Nature
continues to replenish itself. Life is sacred. Man's love for
virtue and for the earth would change its vibration, and
the stars would bless the happy planet below.

What we need to do is overcome self-imposed limitations. They are not of love or God; they are of the perversity of thinking that we learn in schools. There is no truth
in them. It is time for us to outgrow immature thinking
and be human beings rather than citizens attached to a
flag. Nationalism produces no true leadership; it is an
assumed, imposed authority based on a pretense.

Pretense is the wrong-mindedness that is taught everywhere. Harmony has its own potentials and is the fruit of
goodness. We know little of the Love that sustains life or
of Divine Intelligence. Is not falseness to oneself a curse?
When will we ever awaken from . . . *the sleep of forgetfulness*[5] to realize our true Identity? How few are awakened
from within.

There is an inherent joy within each one of us that
lacks nothing, for it is forever grateful. Gratefulness has
yet to sing its songs upon this planet. What are the resources of humanism? What in reality is true productivity
and service? These are the questions we must ask.

Any solutions we pose for America will result in increased unemployment. Even though we have ourselves
trapped, transformation is always possible. But it demands a contact with self-honesty—the space within—
that has the potential to cope with any challenge.

The human being is supreme in Creation. His potentials have no limitation. The action of transformation starts not with seeking but with the undoing of misperceptions and wrong-mindedness. The very problem becomes the solution. Is America willing to abolish war and end poverty upon the planet? If so, then right away we will have to more than double the production of food so that every living being has enough to eat. This would make right use of the technology we have, end the problem of unemployment, and feed the world!

Goodness has its own insight, a link with the universe. True productivity is oriented toward service rather than profit. But in that there is the true gain.

What would be required to make the rural areas of the world self-sufficient? The planet is in need of more vegetation. Growing more food would require roads, bridges, canals for irrigation, hydroelectric dams, and better seeds. It won't lead to the rich getting richer but to enriching mankind. The technology that would be necessary to accomplish this would no longer be wasteful but truly productive.

India was not producing enough food to feed all its people after achieving freedom, even though eighty-five percent of her population lived on the land. In fact, she imported millions of dollars worth of food annually. But the well-organized Rural Community Projects revolutionized agriculture, and in less than a decade, India was exporting food.

India learned that each acre of land could more than double its production, and that irrigating barren earth lets it contribute to the new wealth of a country. As prosperity comes, farmers are able to buy small-scale agricultural machinery. Millions of tractors and water pumps can be sold in tomorrow's world because better agricultural methods will be so desperately needed.

A humanistic approach harmonizes relationships. Reverence allows nature to be true to itself. Once war is abolished and the primary needs are met everywhere simultaneously, we will have ushered in the sanity of a new age upon this planet.

The problem is never external. Man's political systems of today are antiquated. His economic systems are corrupt. His educational systems are barren of ethics or morality. What works is the military. Its technology of destruction is unsurpassed. The outcome of a militaristic approach to life is predictable, for it is contrary to Divine Laws. A loveless practicality is strangling the nation. From the present perspective, in every direction America looks, disaster is around the corner.

Now it even seems the more prosperous a nation is, the more pressured and stimulated. "THE MEEK SHALL INHERIT THE EARTH"[6] is too profound a principle for the intellect to comprehend. It may well be that America cannot afford this new thinking and will hit bottom, for she lacks resilience and serenity. Vested interests have become the enemy. She is not aligned with Universal Laws.

Yet it is possible to rise to wisdom, and undo violence and self-destruction at home as well as abroad. Goodness opens a new vista for America and mankind where reverence and thoughtfulness take precedence. It will come about, whether or not America can rise to merit the opportunity. If she does not, other parts of the world will lead the way. No one can undermine the capacity of the human being. Every living person upon this planet has a precise function.

> *My part is essential*
> *to God's plan for salvation.* [7]

There is enough military equipment—vehicles and planes—to build a better world. Warships could transport food and machinery where they are needed. Jeeps, trucks, and even tanks could be converted initially to serve as tractors. The U.S. Navy could serve in transferring thousands of helpers to go abroad on their peaceful missions, and the sailors could stay for a given time in an area, survey the needs, and help with the building of the means for a new economy, industry, and management. Navy and Army officials could be instructed about the ways and means for carrying out the projects. With no profit or loss, all the information necessary from different quarters of the world could be accessible. That is especially important for governments of poorer nations which have limited understanding of the skills and equipment needed.

Overall, it is a vast project and undertaking. But in the beginning, and at the grassroots level, skills are even more important than costly equipment. One project mastered, or given attention, becomes the model. Once it is understood by American servicemen, they can pass it on to the local areas. It is working with the government and the people of each country—irrespective of their political or economic views, or racial background. The human being is seen as the human being, his belief systems representing his own traditions in which there is no need to interfere.

The personnel of hundreds of American warships could revolutionize a continent because their service would be based on goodwill—not business, or political or religious dogma. For the first time, man goes to help, not to sell or conquer or convert. It is like sharing a new technology, a new science of universal kindness—converting destructive warships to constructive uses. Going to serve rather than to destroy would heighten morality everywhere and transform Americans with its givingness. This action of sanity would help cleanse the heart of man of fear and hostility.

Productivity is basic. Survival depends on it. This relationship of caring could evolve into a world free of war. It would become America to initiate incentives for peace and humanism on the planet.

Such an action could transform the world within a few years—especially if America's heart were in it. Overnight, hundreds of hospitals and dispensaries could arise. Carpenters, potters, and bakers could be taught to produce more efficiently with laborsaving devices. It is important to help these people, but not to take their simplicity away.

We have to protect the underdeveloped areas of the Third World from imitating the overly externalized lifestyles of the West that limit human life to sensation. Sensationalism is an epidemic we need not export.

Resources for these peaceful missions are surely there. It will cost a lot less than the Vietnam and Iraqi Wars, yet it will be a lifesaver—for America, too. All that is needed is the same American enthusiasm and determination exhibited in the U.S. military action of Desert Storm in the Persian Gulf.

Other nations will join and support this noble cause. Reverence for life could be shared by the whole world— no matter what differences there are on other issues. Togetherness would harmonize relationships and lift human morale. America's destiny depends on it. America could be Joseph* for the lean years ahead.

Now that America is the only superpower, her only sane option is to support a war-free world. Otherwise she will destroy herself with domestic problems. Wastefulness has brought poverty to America's doorstep. The price of food could be so low! There is no need for a packet of carrots to cost more than a few cents.

In order to cope with the primary needs of man, we need to think impersonally. Limiting oneself is a contradiction. There is no scarcity where there is non-waste and simplicity. What is required is a total transformation in the premise of our thinking. Our very educational system needs to be revolutionized, being primitive for the most part. Training the brain never soars beyond the body cells. Instead, it stimulates ambition and selfishness. We need not be programmed to obey and to submit.

Education is to awaken the student's vast inner potentials, and not merely confine him to memory. Education, religion, and the politics of self-seeking are deluding mankind by limiting him to the world of appearance. We need to change our values and transform the educational system.

I will not value what is valueless. [8]

This can only be in effect when our education has undergone a renewal. That is the first step—to undo what-

---

*Joseph, a prophet of God in the Old Testament, prepared the Pharaoh in Egypt for the seven lean years. For more about Joseph refer to Chapter 13.

ever assumes false reality and to question the abstract. Education must do more than turn out wage-earners. True education is a sharing where the light of miracles is present. It is not only teaching; it is more an inner awakening.

Our present educational system does not relate the human being to the underlying reality of his divine nature. The universe, when seen by the senses, limits us to appearances. We are often deceived by its outward aspect. Truth is beyond sense perception. Love is a state of being and not an activity of thought.

There is perfect order in the vast universe. Disorder is in the man-made world. Humanity is one. Therefore, the function of education is to relate us to this reality. In actuality there is no past or future—yet we are educated to trust in our distractions from the timeless Present.

Stillness is sacred and as vast as the Present. What is ever present and direct needs no education, only awareness. Nothing is comparable to the innocence of the silent mind of man, and of that we know hardly anything.

The real function of education is to connect us with reality and not to the names we give the world of appearances. Inner awakening requires going beyond the body senses, not personalizing life and limiting ourselves to physicality.

Life is Divine. Perfection, in reality having no lack, need not be sought. It is so; there are no means to it. But the ability to recognize the truth of this is what is missing. We are so preoccupied with the fallacy of activity and self-improvement. The human being, when inconsistent with Divine Law, is detrimental to himself. In his unawareness he interferes with the source of his own being. In a recent letter received from Mother Teresa, she said: "Continue to pray . . . that we may not spoil God's work."

True knowledge is of Eternal Laws. The absolute has no opposite to it. Truth or love or gratefulness or peace of mind or oneness of life cannot be understood by justifying interpretations.

Mass education has gone astray when it teaches *about* truth and not Truth Itself. Yes, we need to learn about our physical self and the physical world; but it is our attachment that brings disorder. Man is part of the perfect order of the universe. His nature is divine. The importance of,

"Know thyself"

cannot be underestimated, nor the wisdom of,

SEEK YE FIRST THE KINGDOM OF GOD,
AND HIS RIGHTEOUSNESS;
AND ALL THESE THINGS
SHALL BE ADDED UNTO YOU.[9]

Rightness seems difficult for most people, but it is simple. There is no complexity in truth. Noncompromise is a power in itself. This power is within each one of us. It is the vitality of truth and uncontaminated compassion. It is the way of love that gives, but wants nothing. The universe responds to the call of an uncompromising man. His integrity fits into no situations and will not conform to circumstances. The wise is not controlled by the external. Selflessness is non-dependent. It is a power in itself. The purity of motiveless life is blessed. Infinite blessing surrounds the unselfish.

The reversal process is from fear to love and goodness. The reversal process from politics to humanism is not an easy transformation to make only if there is resistance. Willingness within to allow rightness to extend will facilitate it. There is no lack of potential, only of goodwill.

It would not take any more ingenuity or funds than having to bear the vast expenditure for military bases around the globe in order to police the world. In reality these are not only unessential but detrimental. Alliances with corrupt dictators contradict every ethic.

The few that profit are even now a formidable force directing America's domestic affairs to their advantage. Money and power concentrated in the hands of the few is largely the source of America's downfall.

Humanity is caught in the problem of possessiveness and insecurity. In the end even the banking system may prove as unreliable as our calculating thoughts. What is reliable is the honest word. The word of goodness is like a seed that is ageless and is accessible to the ear that heeds.

There is much to be done in affluent America while it is still affluent. Urgency is the word. Celestial speedup is upon us. Unemployment, with its surplus workers and machinery, can serve a good purpose. The power of goodness will bring peace to this planet.

To discriminate between Eternal Laws and man-made rules requires an entirely different approach to life, not just another intellectual perspective. Abstract concepts, dogmas, ideas, and belief systems are man-made. They could be termed "educated ignorance," and there is no peace in them. What is Absolute is of God—eternal, changeless, without an opposite—and hence unaffected by anything external. Man-made rules are unreal.

My thoughts are images that I have made. [10]

All things I think I see reflect ideas. [11]

Goodness and gratefulness are eternal attributes of the spirit. Love and truth are Absolute and ever-present. Man-made rules are questionable, but mass education continues to ignore the human being's boundless spiritual potentials.

Awareness of Eternal Laws undoes man-made rules. This is a Law.

My only function is the one God gave me [12]

means that the human being is not subject to the principle of cause and effect, or consequences. His real function is to journey toward truth, having faith in his own integrity, and to live by righteousness—the Law at work in life.

We cannot ignore the significance of spiritual values. The discovery of perfection is denied no one.

Spirit is in a state of grace forever. [13]

Our real nature is Divine. Seeing the fact as a fact liberates us. Peace is of the One Mind of God of which we are all a part.

Where there is integrity there can be no lack. All power is given to man through the Word that created him.

There is tremendous goodwill in America. As mankind moves closer to a life of the spirit, goodness will bring peace to the earth.

> *Your Will can do all things in me,*
> *and then extend to all the world as well through me.*
> *There is no limit on Your Will.*
> *And so all power has been given to Your Son.* [14]

4

"I Am Under No Laws But God's"

The question is—how does the individual undo stimulation and dependence on the system in order to bring order in his own life? And what would it take to make the internal change, make contact with his own divinity, and be a part of Universal Laws? The function of a good society is to produce individuals who outgrow society. As Ralph Waldo Emerson said,

> "What lies behind us and before us are small matters, compared to what lies within us."

It is in America that a new beginning emerges with the advent of *A Course in Miracles*. *A Course In Miracles*, the first scripture to originate in English, has come to awaken man from . . . *the sleep of forgetfulness*,[1] the illusion that life is external. It offers the Thoughts of God as a gift to all mankind. Every sentence of the Course dispels our misperceptions. It declares:

> *Nothing real can be threatened.*
> *Nothing unreal exists.*[2]

Lesson 76 of the *Workbook For Students* reassures us:

> *"I am under no laws but God's."*

We have observed before how many senseless things have seemed to you to be salvation. Each has imprisoned you with laws as senseless as itself. You are not bound by them, yet to understand that this is so, you must first realize salvation lies not there. While you would seek for it in things that have no meaning, you bind yourself to laws that make no sense. Thus do you seek to prove salvation is where it is not. . . .

Think of the freedom in the recognition that you are not bound by all the strange and twisted laws you have set up to save you. You really think that you would starve unless you have stacks of green paper strips and piles of metal discs. You really think a small round pellet or some fluid pushed into your veins through a sharpened needle will ward off disease and death. You really think you are alone unless another body is with you.

It is insanity that thinks these things. You call them laws, and put them under different names in a long catalogue of rituals that have no use and serve no purpose. You think you must obey the laws of medicine, of economics and of health. Protect the body, and you will be saved. . . .

There are no laws except the laws of God. This needs repeating over and over, until you realize it applies to everything that you have made in opposition to God's Will.

Rightness is the strength that overrules one's desire to seek advantage and preference. Certainty follows, as one sees that integrity works. *A Course In Miracles* makes one aware that Life is compassionate. It is gratefulness that lifts man and introduces him to his own sacredness. There is nothing else to learn. The *Course* makes possible the connection with the humanism of our God-created Self.

The premise of the lifestyle of *A Course In Miracles* is of the spirit. In reality, one's holiness is what one shares with another because that is who one truly is.

> *As forgiveness allows love to return to my aware-ness, I will see a world of peace and safety and joy.* [3]

When two people share, there is no lack. Having something of our own to give leads toward service rather than dependence on jobs. In service is our salvation from insecurity and fear of the future. When you are the cause, you affect the externals; when you are an effect, you are externalized. Humanism does not have a program; it merely changes a value within the psyche.

It is not possible to live by certainty and rightness without trust in God. Religion is not intellectual but a state of being upon which time cannot intrude. The *Course* refers to it in Lesson 48:

> *"There is nothing to fear."*

> *The idea for today simply states a fact. It is not a fact to those who believe in illusions, but illusions are not facts. In truth there is nothing to fear. It is very easy to recognize this. But it is very difficult to recognize it for those who want illusions to be true.* [4]

Politics, economy, conventional religion, and institutional education are founded on the abstract world of thought. There is not the sacredness of integrity in it, nor is there loftiness in its nationalism and commerce. It encourages falseness rather than awakening us to our divine nature. Only a motiveless life is free of consequences, for it extends the state that knows no lack.

Before the glow of affluence dims and flickers away let us gladden the heart of humanity for we are One in Life. A new and powerful action can inspire this nation to shining greatness. To make peace, charity, and goodness real is not costly. Givingness has its own resources. Goodwill reverses the process of degeneration. There is no lack where there is moral strength to unleash the full force of humanism. And the urgency is compelling.

Humanism responds to another's need out of its own clarity. It works in every situation, and always has to give. It can end the abuse of men and nations because it sees that exploitation is based on false values. In togetherness we could all survive and meet the primary needs of all mankind.

When we move toward rightness, order, and inner awareness, benevolent forces are there to help us. Everything is really secondary to our own inner awakening, for only in awakening will we find our function. Each of us needs friendship with wisdom. This is what the world has lost. We must rise to the Love of God within us, to the remembrance that we are One.

When one is disillusioned with the externals, there is no choice but to find the strength within. Everything else will fail—but the potentials of one's own sacredness are boundless.

PART II

THE

AWAKENING

*The Kingdom is perfectly united
and perfectly protected,
and the ego will not prevail against it.
Amen.* [1]

*There is a point
beyond which illusions cannot go.* [2]

The Human Crisis—
The Gap Is Increasing

A city, the highly adored pride of nations, is in itself an enlarged ego. Is this ego enlarged as a mechanism of self-preservation and self-interest?

There is only one Source of life. Everything that lives extends and expands. For example, the tree produces a whole crop of seeds and is consistent with this law. The love and truth that sustain life are our perfection to extend.

In our state of separation from one another we cannot create, but we can project and give value to what we make. Therefore, we suffer from our own misperceptions. The city is a child of our inner separation. Through the isolation of fear and anxiety, the city extends and expands our separation from nature. Knowing this we must realize the implications of what we have initiated.

The slums of New York City will not only continue, they will get worse, regardless of riches the city might amass. Drugs and violence will proliferate no matter how much the city or the Federal Government tries to contain them. The gap between the rich and the poor is widening and there will be slums of staggering proportions. Since growth and expansion will not stop, war is inevitable. It is the industrial economy's most profitable solution and quite acceptable to the collective consciousness.

Industrialists, political leaders, heads of organized religions, and militarists think alike, for the secondary man is in the forefront, having in his power the ability to drain human energy into a "King Kong" of affluence. It is an artificial affluence. Without peace within we are caught in a world of appearances—the slavery of separation from our Source. A collective consciousness that is limited to physical sensation can be exploited. The system can improve and even perfect technology, but slums are its creation as well. Affluence and decadence go hand in hand.

BUT TO THE SEER ALONE,
THE EFFECTS UNFOLD THE
INVISIBLE CAUSE.

The city is by nature seductive, and in the long run self-destructive, for it is unnatural. We see this in the large number of people who congregate in one area. A concentrated city of ten million people, with no farm land surrounding it, is dependent on transportation for food from faraway places, the transportation often costing more than the product itself. It is not the city that sustains the human being but the countryside with its ever-productive earth. And some day the waste of human energy will catch up.

Skyscrapers, owned by rich corporations, are built with human energy. Yet the human being does not have a place of his own. The trend now is to own a car and to work for another rather than to own a home. Without a home children grow up without roots. What could be more important than the individual and sociological atmosphere of a home, where children can grow up with gardens and flower beds of their own? It would be a place for reunion, a place to be in the sunlight with the songs of birds and friends. A law providing every citizen with a home—so that there are no tenants—would bring about a system of newness, consistent with the New World consciousness.

Outrageous, you may say, all the while approving of the corporate skyscrapers and profiteers with incomes as great as some of the nations of the world. The wealth they have amassed is phenomenal; they virtually own the sky, the oceans, and the earth, along with the human beings who live upon it. Certainly we can afford to give children a place to establish their roots so their parents are not haunted by the monthly rent that compels them to be wage-earners. Insecurity produces careers that prevent the intrinsic expression of one's Beingness. Most of the population today produces unessential things.

The city is built by exploitative minds. They subject themselves—and all of us—to the dictates of "thought, then action," with a wide gap in between sustained by the energy of conflict.

The city is where the personality ordeal is all-consuming. Simplicity is annihilated by dependence. Stimulation dominates our lives and influences our choices of food, profession, and relationships. It subjects us to habit and sensation. In the absence of relaxation and serenity, our activities are dominated by the quest for survival and gratification; our pursuit of pleasure is in direct relationship to our increasing sense of insecurity and fear. An artificial life of conflict attempts to escape from fear through pleasure.

"Bigness" is sustained by accelerated growth. The consequences of this acceleration are alarming. It is self-destructive. The industrial empire spreads by first arousing appetites and then by appeasing those appetites with manufactured products. Thus, one always needs money. And so the gap between nations, between the "haves" and the "have-nots," widens.

There is another ever-widening gap that is even more sinister: the gap between the average person and those who have control over him. The electronic technology of vested interests is so swift and imperceptible in its subliminal effects that the layperson is taken in without knowing it. The commercial world has its illusionary territorial rights over the populace.

This is more serious than we realize. It is not only an abuse of nature or an exploitation of markets, it is a manipulation of the human being himself. Henry James said, "I am often struck at the limitation with which men of power pay the price for their domination over mankind."

More and more we are being limited to the "known," to the appetites and the bondage of physicality. Our function is limited to mere routine. We are enslaved by the industrial economy. As this invasion upon our freedom continues, something natural—the spontaneous within us —is being destroyed.

Violation on such a massive scale brings an unforeseen contamination of human consciousness which affects the very atmosphere that surrounds the earth. The crust of the earth and human consciousness are related. The thin layer that surrounds the globe where life exists is an extension of human consciousness and is affected by it.

Even our ability to question is becoming limited. Our choices fall within the realm of duality. In this most affluent society most people are woefully low on money and thus confined to their milieu. Education, for the most part, prepares us to fit in and serve the system. How many of us are confined to being wage earners? Banks, telephone companies, and insurance corporations have the last word.

In the city, where nearly everyone is an employee, few can afford a home. But the nation can afford war and aggression! The city can afford tobacco companies but not "LOVE YE ONE ANOTHER."[1] Tobacco companies can afford to provide hundreds of parks, avenues of flower beds, and trees. Instead, cigarettes are the main crop of the city. What, then, is our affluence? Is it not what Henry David Thoreau called,

". . . improved means to an unimproved end"?

Let us heed the farsighted words of Abraham Lincoln:

"Prosperity breeds tyrants."

Our perception is either true or false. But do we not see how discernment, the most valuable gift of Heaven, is taken away from us and we do not even know it?

God did not create a meaningless world.[2]

For generations people have been made helpless by their lack of awareness of the purity of all-knowing Innocence. Innocence is too wise to get tangled up in the ways of man. It knows God as the Creator, the Father, the creative Force behind manifestation, the Sustainer of life, the Light beyond perception.

I want to point out that I am not speaking of socialism, communism, or capitalism. These are man-made. My primary interest is in man's relationship with his eternal Self, not his economic or political views. Of course, external conditions are important and cannot be underestimated; but the Source of physical senses is divine to me.

Having come from India to America I was all too aware that it is a fallacy to seek political peace without having internal peace. The discovery of the impact of science on society was vital to me.

Humanity's instinctive nature is good. Of this I had no doubt. Since I saw all people as good I could not accept the "enemy" as bad. My concern was with the factors that mislead us, for once confused, our clarity is lost. I saw that life was too externalized and that the media generated influence and increased misinformation. The daily newspapers fostered a hysteria, fear, and frustration, and contributed to our imbalances. The media and its propaganda were very commercial.

I questioned prosperity. Did it increase or decrease the distance between man and his divine nature? Did science and prosperity contribute to virtue, ethics, or the dignity of man? I wondered if better relationships between the nations of the East and the West would help. In fact, this later became a passion with me and brought me in contact with men and women whose lives were intrinsic and who valued the goodness of man. Peace and goodness are not found outside oneself and then brought in; what is within us reaches out and beyond.

I view man as a co-creator with God. The planet welcomes his presence, which brings to it the vibration of the Kingdom of Heaven. Man-made rules and values are "horizontal." I am looking at the "vertical" man who is pressured to conform in this so-called land of new consciousness.

Although I have been to almost all of the great cities of the world, I am not comparing. Direct comprehension does not compare. Mine is a question. In what way is the New World new? According to Divine Law, everything extends itself. Where is the thinking that originates from the creativity of love and peace, or from the Mind of God? In what way has the New World awakened to, "THY WILL BE DONE ON EARTH AS IT IS IN HEAVEN"?[3]

Here in the New World, as elsewhere, we are caught in the self-centeredness of the images of thought preoccupied with survival. Even our educational institutions and organized religions are sustained by the energy of friction, based as they are on limited, physical senses. They do not awaken us to wholeness. Yet love is the law.

Our inner purity changes all circumstances; we are not helpless. Nothing external can control us. As long as we try to exploit another, however, we violate the Eternal Law and are subject to consequences. How expensive the consequences have become!

"Let us have faith that right makes might, and in that faith, let us, to the end, dare to do our duty . . .

"Let us strive to deserve . . . the continued care of Divine Providence, trusting that, in future

national emergencies, He will not fail to provide
us the instruments of safety and security.

"Destroy that spirit, and you have planted the
seeds of despotism around your own doors."

ABRAHAM LINCOLN

These words, then, are not political. They are the statement of a vertical man who is not swayed by circumstances.

Agrarian societies produced saints in ancient times
and urban civilization has produced geniuses of the creative arts. But the vast majority of the population has
remained subject to conformity.

"Yesterday" and "tomorrow" are projections of the
human brain and are not a reality at all. Whether we are
in the city or in the village we live by the same misconcep-
tions. We can see the similarity behind their obvious differences.

We have dwelt enough on the city and on the pastoral
lifestyle of the rural communities. Now, outgrowing both
village and city is our primary concern. The important
thing is man's discovery of himself and his identity with
God. This makes the external issues secondary. Whether
rural or urban, the life of external preferences is common
to both. The fact is, however, where there is choice, there
is no freedom. Self-centeredness is the origin of contradiction and conflict upon the planet.

We need to establish the very foundation and purpose
for our being on the earth. And we need to take the stand
that will end the separation between man and man and

between man and God; and come to the union, the wholeness of the One Life we all share.

PRESENT IS PRESENT.

GOD IS.

YOU ARE NOT SEPARATED, BUT INDEPENDENT, AS LOVE IS INDEPENDENT.

Cities and villages of the world are caught in the mis-
conceptions of solving the self-created problems of insecurity and separation. What has man's culture done to
bring the individual to the peace of God or the reality of
the Light that he is? What is so lofty about any culture that
drafts its citizens to wage war and uses its economy as a
means of self-destruction?

Fortunately, ignorance is not eternal. People today, as
harassed as we are by unfulfillment and its consequences,
can surely outgrow the illusion of external nothingness.
Time has no effect on our eternity. Nor are we any less
holy than as God created us. Love cannot be afraid. Its
radiance rekindles and increases in joy. Natural intelligence is effortless. It is not timebound.

Our personality is conditioned, but it has no power
over our eternity. Unless we surrender to it. The choice is
ours.

Knowing you are sustained by the Love of God, you,
too, out of the gratefulness of your heart, can join the
chorus of everything in creation singing the glory of its
own perfection in praise of the Creator.

6

America's Destiny—Humanism

An Indian villager does not visit psychologists or lawyers when he has a problem. He goes to a saint or holy person, a relative or a neighbor who is at peace. Such persons have values beyond "me and mine," and when he talks with them something is shared which is not limited to the personal. Although there is not much money in that part of the world, there is humanism.

In the evening you could go for a walk together in the fields. Lovingly your friend would then invite you to talk saying, "Come. Sit down." Whatever your concerns, they would be dissolved. Being "backward," sometimes the villagers are unaware even of who the Prime Minister is, but they can be very wise. "God is our ruler," they would state, "these others come and go."

Instead of producing politicians, such a country brings forth leaders who are giants of ethics and values. Several of these wise men of intrinsic life and consistent knowledge made a strong impact on my life. One of the most extraordinary was Gianiji Kartar Singh. I met him on a train at Amritsar on the way to Lahore in 1945.

He came and sat opposite me in the compartment. I was in crisis, burning to make contact and not knowing how to approach him. But the energy of first thought acts involuntarily. Gianiji, an eminent man, was the leader of the Sikhs. His Sikhism encompassed all humanity in its range; his nationalism was unlimited humanism.

Gianiji was a man of renunciation and religious outlook who never had a bank account. His life was completely simple and given to service. It is he who taught me humanism. The force of his love transformed my life, and in his atmosphere I blossomed. He offered an intimate relationship through which I became a friend of Prime Minister Nehru and others of incorruptible lives. When people asked him, "What do you see in Tara Singh?" Gianiji would say:

"The word 'impossible' does not apply to him.
He will not accept second best and this will
make him or break him."

This contact with the wise opened totally new dimensions and potentials within me and made things possible in an India besieged by the cruelty of poverty. It culminated in an enormous industrial project at the grassroots level with capital of over six million dollars supported by Sikhs, maharajahs, and others—but most of all by Gianiji's impeccable integrity.

In 1947, however, the advent of freedom and the partition of India and Pakistan disrupted this humanistic plan. Before embarking upon another venture I felt the need to visit the West to make an individual survey of the impact of science on society. One questioned what part the world's underdeveloped, agrarian society of almost two billion was to play in the Post-War period.

When the British granted India its freedom the wise were asked to formulate its Constitution, and an untouchable was made the head of the committee. Gianiji led the constitutional committee on minorities and democracy; I was one of his assistants. We studied the examples of Switzerland and French Quebec to find ways of dealing with these issues.

Before coming to America one had discovered how the British exploited the colonies. But so did the native Indian kings, or maharajahs. Five million Indians died of starvation in the early 1900s. "Wages are going down instead of up," wrote Swami Rama Tirtha, "notwithstanding the increase of industries, the extension of railway systems, and other sources of wealth and employment that are being rapidly developed."[1]

Britain demanded more from India than the country could give, and so the colony's debt rose from 51 million pounds in 1857 to 200 million in 1901. Its resources were taken, the people starved, and the nation was put under debt.

People have been exploited from the beginning of time. That is the very nature of society—regardless of whether it is affluent or poor. There have also been many attempts at reform, however. Communism was the hope of the world at one time, but the only solution would lie in decentralization of power and control. Decentralization has been tried time and time again but those who bring it into effect then concentrate power into their own hands.

Working with Gianiji I had seen the exploitation both by the British and the maharajahs. Then I came to America because it was the leader of the world. She had the potentials to start a new order based on humanism, not politics or dogmas. So Life brought me to America to see the impact of science on society and to show that humanism is the answer—not reaction or militarism.

In reality there is no America. People came to this continent from different countries of the world, and they met. Some native tribes had lived here for many thousands of years before the others came. The experiment was— how would they relate with each other? Would they share the bounty in this New World?

People came to the New World with hope; it was a step away from Europe's feudalism and the tyranny of religions. But as the world's downtrodden came to this rich land they could not contain themselves. The Gold Rush was as destructive for the white man as alcohol was for the American Indian. As early as 1838, Ralph Waldo Emerson gravely assessed:

> "This country has not fulfilled what seemed the reasonable expectation of mankind."

America developed a culture based on seeking external glamour while belittling internal values and principles.

Progress thus offered only increased efficiency. Our education consisted of gaining skills—which allowed us to better compete but we forfeited peace in the process. The law of "might is right" rules in a career-oriented society which always seeks greater competence at gaining advantage for itself. Where man lives by attachment and the unfulfillment of body senses, violence flourishes.

Man, with all his knowledge, is imprisoned in his own world of abstract thought-images. In his quest to train his brain he has neglected and overlooked self-discovery and the spaciousness of serenity. The true purpose of education was to introduce the human being to his vast potentials. We disregard the potential and just train the brain to do routine work like a machine.

We run away from innocence and then need a drink to forget our anxieties. Today every home is crowded with unnecessary things. Simplicity and wisdom are rare; self-forgetfulness has become an absolute necessity.

In America today the small farmer can hardly hold his own against large corporate landowners. And because of his dependence on gasoline and mechanization he does not even have the resources to be self-reliant should gasoline become scarce. We have contaminated the earth and it is becoming almost impossible to restore the necessary balance. We have interfered with just about everything that is natural—food, clothing, animals, and the earth itself.

It is not only in the production of armament that powerful commercial interests ignore consequences for mankind. Some of the policies and practices that increase profits for the food and drug industries in America also increase suffering for the human being.

In his book, *Diet For A New America*, John Robbins states:

"Our environment and food chains are being inundated by a virtual avalanche of pesticides. What three decades ago took us six years to produce, we now produce every couple of hours.

"But the very poisonous and persistent qualities of these toxic chemicals have made them big money-makers for the chemical companies who market them aggressively. These corporations have applied enormous political and economic pressure to keep their products in use. The tragic result is that millions of pounds of these lethal agents continue to be used every year."[2]

Citing a National Cancer Institute study, he points out:

"In 1900, cancer was the tenth leading cause of death in the United States, and was responsible for only three percent of all deaths. Today, it ranks second, and causes about twenty percent of all deaths. More Americans will die of cancer *this year* than died in World War II, the Korean and the Vietnamese wars combined.

"Forty years ago, cancer in children was a medical rarity. Today, more children die of cancer than from any other cause.

"Many scientists now feel that the presence of toxic chemicals in our bodies is largely responsible for these epidemics."[3]

Democracy or anything else man-made—no matter how good it seems to be—will end up working things to its own advantage. No matter how lofty its beginning, everything degenerates that is of thought and time. Politics, religion, education, and science always follow that law. When you realize this is so, you turn within and say, "I will not work under the authority of another."

Human beings are not important to governments. Whether communistic or capitalistic, their goals are exactly the same—military might and industrial economies. But there is a different way—that way is humanism.

Following World War II the planet was divided into three camps. One was the West—composed of the Americas and Western Europe. Communist countries formed the second group, including the Soviet Union and the Eastern European nations. Finally, about two billion subsistence farmers made up the Third World. These village dwellers were usually poor, illiterate, and unconcerned with politics.

Most of the world's human energy and resources were in the Third World. These underdeveloped nations had abundant natural resources but needed technological help in order to develop them. Many had been colonies that were exploited by the Western industrialized nations and drained of their natural wealth. A new world order was emerging, and colonies were receiving their independence as the ruling European nations could no longer retain control after the stresses of the Second World War.

My survey of America involved making serious inquiry. How would the world's leading nation—America—relate with this mass of human energy, this resource of two billion people? Could she aspire to question the validity of "might is right" and rise to the opportunity of seeing the world as one humanity? Or would her vested interests prevail and focus the nation's economy on military might, leaving the problem of starvation unresolved?

Generations of deprivation had left the Third World with great, crying needs. But it had humanism to offer the West. Over 40,000 leaders of India went to prison while non-violently seeking the country's independence. Some

17,000 women courted imprisonment by breaking unjust British colonial laws that taxed salt, the poor man's necessity. Seventy thousand Indian men protested against the British government in the first Salt March and were sent to jail. Moral issues were of first importance to them. Mahatma Gandhi said, "We will not correct wrong with over-doing of wrong."

When brought to trial for supporting impoverished peasants, Gandhi said to the magistrate, "The only course open to you is . . . either to resign your post, or inflict on me the severest penalty, if you believe that the system and law you are assisting to administer are good for the people." Gandhi represented the goodness of humanism. Out of his caring he spoke to what is eternal in man. His was an impersonal action. Gandhi was not interested in politics but in helping end man's misery.

Given that background I was shocked to see that America was bitter about communism, which is only an abstract idea. When confronted with an actual offense, Gandhi would say, "The enemy is not always wrong. I have no personal ill-will against a single administrator, much less can I have any disaffection towards the King's person. But I hold it a virtue to be disaffected towards a Government which in its totality has done more harm to India than any previous system." Wisdom lies in weeding out animosity and becoming objective. Nothing derailed Gandhi's peace. Why should Americans find rising above their own reactions to be so difficult?

Humanism is unchanging—it relates man to what is not of time in himself. Humanism is religious; it offers pure politics, pure skills, and pure intelligence. Humanism is not primitive, for it uplifts the spirit of the planet and introduces man to his higher nature.

The action of humanism was and is needed in this country. But we always tend to think it is the rest of the world that needs something from America. Our industrial power could improve the lot of man, and free him from the drudgery of manual labor. Can America now respect humanism and help the human being on the planet? To do so, we will have to make corrections in our political system.

How many millions of dollars does it take to be elected to office? Anyone who does not have that kind of money is left out. Where is democracy when only a small percentage of people can afford to give expression to their aspiration? Democracy in its pure spirit is humanism. When humanism is absent, there is no democracy.

The lower side of man is of the earth. In the struggle for survival and territory, violence is natural. Militarism predominates when man thinks he is merely of the earth. In actuality he is an eternal spirit, capable of rising to a humane perspective. Nationalism represents the law of might. Nationalism wants more claws and fangs—deadlier weapons. Militarizing the planet may be good for industrial economies, but where is the sanity in it?

There is much wastefulness in wrong thinking, as well as dire consequences. The fact is that only wisdom and rightness are free of consequences. Humanism wants to say, "Listen, that's not the way." And somehow, when I came to this country, I was in contact with that force, and represented it. I had not come to earn money but to volunteer my services. And in this materialistic society I almost starved. Even when the money ran out, I would not compromise and work for another. Self-reliance is an experiment one lived by.

I had wondered if there was space for humanism in the New World. And there was the sense that if it did not go in that direction it would self-destruct. Aldous Huxley said that evil, unable to resist temptation, in the end destroys itself. Being the war's victor nation, the path America chose had an enormous impact on mankind everywhere.

Worldwide overpopulation and illiteracy were two of the many problems after World War II. America's technology could have helped by putting its industrial might and skills to right use. With wisdom, farsightedness, and the spirit of humanism, America could have turned the tide in the world. Had that been done, America would have flourished. But now she will suffer the consequences for having been indifferent to people in sorrow and in need. An opportunity was lost to come to rightness—to discover the spirit of helpfulness and caring—and in doing so, replenish the earth.

WHAT IS HUMANISM?

Communism could not compete with the West after World War II, the Soviet Union alone having lost over 20 million lives and with much of the country in devastation. America's fear could have been avoided through adopting a different approach. If America had used its resources to be the world leader in dealing with problems of human deprivation, how could it ever lack friends?

Humanism would have said, "We do not care what your beliefs and traditions are. America is here to share technology, build better roads, generate electricity, and lead nations to self-reliance. We want to extend goodwill and end poverty and starvation in the world."

Overpopulation, primitive agricultural practices, and poor health care could not be corrected by the Third World. Adequate resources were not available at the national level. Only at the level of humanity could such problems be solved.

I visited the Soviet Union in 1958, and there was not an anti-American feeling there. In America there was hardly a single person who was not contaminated with the suspicion of communism. Communism and capitalism are really no different, for neither produces a change in values. America's superior position was due simply to the fact that her industry and technology were 30 or 40 years ahead of Russia's after World War II. It is probable that Russia's friendship could have been won without superpower competition.

Then what fear was it that drove America to burn its wheat and throw potatoes into the ocean by the tons? One began to see that not only was there paranoia about communism but an insanity that would waste food when there was famine in the world. This fear would at some point destroy America. The divisiveness it has created in the world is also present within, and will become more and more apparent as stresses in society increase.

What is it we have to give that is not of this world? America's political, military, and economic successes will be harmful in the end if their source is wrong-mindedness. One can become weakened even while being externally strong.

Being an extension of humanism at the age of twenty-seven allowed one to come into contact with a handful of superb people who had objective viewpoints and who made decisions at a high level. In principle they agreed with what I said but there was not much they could do. Although they were Supreme Court Justices and Senators, they were not in charge of America and their voices were not heard. When I met them they explained, "If you have a sane view, you become as if exiled."

No longer are such persons advisers to Cabinet members, for those positions now are political in nature. Today the larger view is not accessible to decision-makers, nor is it reported by the media.

I found that individuals are good, but the system degrades them. The pressure people are under in this technological society will destroy them. As stress increases, morality and ethics deteriorate. That is happening the world over and it is driving people to self-destruction. No one has the space for simplicity.

When I would talk to the Rockefeller Foundation or the leaders behind the Point Four Program, they would say, "You're a good man. You should be ambassador." Then they would suggest someone else for me to go see.

After talking with other people one would go back and say, "I don't want to see anyone else. I've come to see you. What is it that you are willing to do?" Matters would stop there. "Humanism is good—peace is good—but we're in business," would be the answer.

Businesses did not want to invest in Asia. They would refer you to the Red Cross or the Carnegie Foundation for aid. But what the world needed was new wealth. American capital did not want to go to poor countries because it could earn more here. It could make immense profits by manufacturing potato chips or some other unessential goods. Why should it go to Burma? It did not even want to go to Canada. Instead, profits could be gained by increasing publicity here through television, radio—even T-shirts.

America destroys food to obey the laws of commerce since vested interests control the lobbying system and the government. Industry could have developed markets for its goods in the Third World instead of putting more and more human energy and money into the manufacture of arms and the securing of military bases around the world.

Weapons are instruments of destruction while tractors and water pumps produce food and help humanity. Trillions of dollars which we invested in weapons did not in turn produce anything. What an opportunity there was for America to extend reverence for Life, and have the strength of rightness that would ennoble its people. There are consequences for putting energy into destroying life rather than into protecting it. One day we may discover that devoting resources to unproductive armaments leads to bankruptcy. Self-centered economic progress is a form of savagery. It is territorial, and dependent upon "might makes right."

Humanism offers a contact with your own integrity— a different kind of sensitivity which is not personal. It has no prejudice, a condition which nationalism will not allow. It makes no conclusions about another or how a situation should or should not be. For humanism, what is, is.

Humanism is not schooled. Nor is it a skill, for it is not survival-oriented. Thus it is independent of the physical senses and their illusions. Humanism is not mental. You cannot fit it into the known, for humanism has no beliefs, no conclusions, and no past conditioning. It is the light of attention, free from the seeking of results. Humanism offers a way of life that is free from consequences, for it has no motives.

Humanism is a state of being which is whole and established in itself. It is an unchangeable cause, not an effect. Being related to Life, humanism is natural, free of outside influences and abstract ideas.

Humanism is aware and deals solely with the actual. Those who are with it do not make it a cause, for it cannot be organized. Humanism is not an activity or it becomes organized politics or religion. It introduces one to the involuntary, spontaneous action of Life. It is the shared joy of God and goodness with one another.

Humanism awakens the responsibility of being a human being, not a citizen, since Life is divine. It will not fit into conformity, which represents violence and the memory of yesterday. It is the everlasting reality of the present moment, ever new.

Humanism is of awakened awareness, not educated brain cells. It is a vision of the peace and joy of simplicity, independent of educated dogma and institutional beliefs which promote separation.

Man is controlled and pressured by his education to belong to the traditional system's conformity. Transformation thus is almost impossible, for there is not the Kingdom of Heaven's undivided sacredness in man-made society. There is not the space for the human being to be with his own contentment. Humanism is more valuable than all the education and all the arts in the world. It is what brought one to America.

7

Affluence Without Wisdom
Is Self-Destructive

Wisdom makes one humane. Intellectual learning makes one self-centered. The focus of learning is on improving the personality—which our educational system caters to. But an education of wisdom undoes the primitive and the old within ourselves. Our present educational system merely extends the tradition of yesterday.

As we become more self-centered there is less space for leisure, wisdom, and peace. Pretty soon we are going the way of consequences because we do not know any other. But we have learned all kinds of ways to *postpone* consequences. If there is a health problem, modern medicine invents injections and pills for dealing with it. And doctors even know the side effects the medicines will have and what to do for those. So nothing ever ends; it just shifts.

Our momentum of learning is an evasion. It does not correct errors, it just tries to hoodwink them. Self-interest is always present. In India the wise people say that you cannot change the basic element of something. You can take gold and make earrings with it. Or you can make a bracelet or rings out of it. You can even smash it up. But it is still gold—the form doesn't matter. Content matters.

Learning is almost always selfish. Focusing on "me and mine" divides man from man, because it is contrary to wholeness. It perpetuates separation and intensifies conflict. Friction and violence continue. And no one wants to cure it even though everyone wants to talk about it. Finally, learning comes up with the notion: "peace through war."

One's first impression of America was that it was clean, efficient, and dependable. Customs officials were not corrupt; nor was the salesman going to try to cheat you. People were healthy and prosperous. Hot and cold water, gas, and electricity all were at your fingertips. Cars and gasoline were inexpensive. One could buy food without worrying about cleanliness, or manufactured goods without being concerned about reliability. Getting on a turnpike, one could not have imagined the efficiency. Even trees were planted along the highway. It was easy to love America.

When you went to the United Nations, what the speaker said immediately was translated into many different languages. One was astonished by what man had accomplished. Even in terms of thoughtfulness America excelled. Meters were in taxis so that passengers would not have to argue with the drivers over fares.

Because the standard of living was high you could trust people. In India if you took your laundry to someone he might tell you to come back for it in a week. But if a wedding took place within the next few days the laundry man might go wearing your shirt.

America was the first nation I had heard of where the government belonged to the people. Government programs helped citizens get homes; the GI Bill helped provide education. This was a friendly government, which is a very rare thing.

But there were also many contradictions: the slums of Harlem and the Statue of Liberty shocked me. Men subject to a constitution are not free—that is a denial of Universal Law. Any civilization that puts the primary needs of man in the second place is unwise. Its thinking is based on false and wrong values. Problems of deprivation in an industrial age are unthinkable from a humanistic point of view. When would America rise to maturity?

Right after World War II Egyptian President Nasser told the U.S. that his country wanted friendship and trade but that it would not provide military bases. "Our war is against poverty," explained President Nasser.

America could have fostered a culture in which goodness was more important than dogma. Without goodness the higher part of man does not surface. Goodness offers harmony and peace, for it demands adherence to different values. It changes the educational system and social life, while keeping the indulgence and outlets of the industrialized world in check. Goodness is good for every nation, and all mankind could contribute. In a regional world of differences, there would be a universal outlook.

Without goodness and harmony the very lure of prosperity deceives man, and leads him to degeneration. America now has an impressive collection of outlets and indulgences, but humanity cannot survive without wisdom and simplicity. Man's brain has invented the finest and most advanced commodities, but the inner man is lonely, afraid, panicky.

"There are different kinds of poverty. In India
some people live and die in hunger. There, even
a handful of rice is precious. . . .

"But in the West you have another kind of poverty, spiritual poverty. This is far worse. . . . You
have the poverty of people who are dissatisfied
with what they have, who do not know how to
suffer, who give in to despair. This poverty of
heart is often more difficult to relieve and to
defeat. In the West you have many more broken
homes, neglected children, and divorce on a
huge scale." [1]   MOTHER TERESA

It was shocking to see how nationalism prevents the
goodness within from arising, and how affluence becomes
a real block in the discovery of man's potential. Sheer
affluence does not enrich man. Divorce rates keep going
up, and fashions change yearly as though everyone is regulated by someone else.

I watched the United Nations at work. There was no
hope for it to succeed. Some of its agencies were beneficial,
yes, but it did not fully represent the spirit of humanism.
For the most part its interests were nationalistic. The U.N.
was dominated by bickering between the two veto-wielding
superpowers and would not take bold steps such as limiting
the military budgets of all nations. Supposedly, the function
of the United Nations was to settle international disputes.
There was also the World Court that could have resolved
the boundary disputes between the Arabs and the Israelis.
But when the superpowers take sides the policy of divide-
and-rule prevails. It is a choice between justice and vested
interests.

Nationalism is controlled by those who see violence as a solution. And the populace accepts this. Such a country's educational system might be advanced but it will still be primitive in terms of helping man advance. Politicians will speak out against some dictators but become friends with others. "How does that happen?" I wondered. It was like a child who trusts his parents only to find that his faith is unmerited. None of the politicians were statesmen and there were hardly any unbiased voices.

I did encounter a small minority of Americans who were objective. Over the years, however, it became apparent this was insufficient in proportion to the mass of society with lower values. The only way to rise to this nobleness—this goodness—is through the strength of rightness and virtue. But in America, where almost everything is left to man-made rules and to the police, wisdom, simplicity, and non-waste are ignored. The system promotes a belief in tanks and nuclear missiles, not in the power of goodness within each person.

As man loses contact with Eternal Laws, fear intensifies. Today the "best" technology is devoted to destructive means. And it will bring the land to bankruptcy. When a country is strong because it has worked everything in its own favor, will it ever listen to a call for wisdom? America neglected the Navajo, the Hopi, the Cherokee, the Sioux, and others—how is she going to pursue humanism now? Emerson said:

> "One would think from the talk of men that riches and poverty were a great matter; and our civilization mainly respects it. But the Indians say that they do not think the white man, with his brow of care, always toiling, afraid of heat

and cold, and keeping within doors, has any
advantage of them."

How great a contribution Native Americans could
have made had they not been eliminated from the land
with which they had lived in harmony for tens of thousands of years. Now we lack the wisdom they were to have
imparted to the world.

Will America be able to cope with becoming a secondary power? Rampant violence will emerge, and the police
will be given even more control.

Immorality is what makes a person inwardly weak.
How can any country burn wheat and dump tons of
potatoes in the ocean—rather than giving the food to
poor nations—in order to protect agricultural prices?

An estimated 40,000 infants die each day in the Third
World from nutritional stress and infectious disease. Two
billion people today do not have clean water for drinking.

As vast as these problems are, what is spent on just one
spaceship or nuclear submarine would go a long way toward protecting human lives. Each day America spends
over $3.50 per citizen on defense while about one billion
people in the world *live* on one dollar a day. Most of them
are under age fifteen, and many will die before reaching
age five.

When this country is doing the wrong thing, the fear
of communism—or some other "ism"—intensifies. But
there is no communism if one is doing the right thing. It
is due to lack of humanism that problems arise. Where
there is humanism, a nation helps the world build better

roads, hospitals, schools, and canals. Would there not be a blessing upon this planet if all of humanity had food to eat? How could we not be glorified as a nation for doing so?

Humanism is a virtuous way of life. It demands a profound change of values and inner transformation. The world's present system of education, business, and technology has no need for it.

There was great generosity in America after World War II. The Point Four Program and the work of many philanthropic organizations was unprecedented; there was much goodwill. Years before, America had the foresight to grant tax breaks for charitable contributions, and many wealthy families and corporations established foundations, including the Carnegies, Rockefellers, Ford, and General Motors. They did tremendous good and their administrators were wonderful people. Religious groups such as the Quakers also had extraordinary reputations for their moral character and benevolent work.

But one discovered that the philanthropic expression was not in proportion to the problem. America led the world in such aid but few recognized that philanthropy dealt largely with emergencies. It helped when there were floods, earthquakes, and famines. Afterward, however, conditions were usually just as they were before the disaster.

What would one have to do in order to be a cause that affects a change? Sustained cooperation and capital in the billions of dollars would be required to create a new wealth in Third World countries. When wells are dug to supply more water, and better seeds and farm equipment introduced, the land starts to produce more crops. Then people have the resources to stand on their own feet at all times. They would be building strength on their own territory rather than becoming dependent on charity.

American industry could have found ample markets in the Third World. This nation would have been no poorer for raising the living standards of other nations. America's integrity could have caused a change of values in the world, bringing an end to the fear and exploitation of another. But the war on communism made government aid more and more subject to politics. Countries which agreed with America, and mostly those that allowed military bases, got the help.

What happened then was that the poor people in the newly-freed colonies got impatient. They became restless when they did not see their situation improving. And one by one governments collapsed in the countries of Asia, Africa, and South America. Rule, for the most part, was taken over by military leadership.

America's global policy was to contain communism, not to harm other countries. Yet when one nation received U.S. military aid, neighboring countries were usually forced to respond in kind. From 1954 to 1963 America spent $1 billion arming and training Pakistani forces. In the face of this growing strength, India was compelled to divert funds meant for the primary needs of man to its military.

Within this country itself, why is there not a Hopi Congressman or Senator? Who represents those people? Is variety encouraged? Is there toleration of differences?

What if there was a real demand that children in schools be taught not to waste? What if Congress passed a law forcing companies which manufacture cans to keep the land litter-free and to recycle the empties? Can America not afford wisdom?

Why are there no laws concerning the violence on television which is perverting children? There is a gun in almost every child's hand. You would think that mothers would protest.

Why is it rare for Americans to take a stand on moral grounds? Is the only time someone stands up when they are asking for higher wages? You do not find thousands of people here going to jail for ethical reasons. And even if a protest march or other event takes place, its effect is limited due to the impact of the mass media. Most of the news is sensational because reporters go to the hospitals and police stations to report on accidents and crime. Every day there are new stories of violence and the public has become immune to shock.

Modern media offers an innumerable variety of distractions. This makes it very difficult to find peace within —or even to find the space which sees the need for peace within.

Children get introduced to these distractions at a young age. This makes it difficult for them to heed the intrinsic call within to their life's real purpose. American democracy offers outlets instead: a circus of choices justified by "I do as I please." Thus, man degenerates, losing his integrity and universality. We are left with pervasive waste and much loneliness.

It is almost impossible today to be free of influences and beliefs. Even though profits and nationalism do not offer freedom, the simplicity of wisdom has little appeal for most people. Pure action of the spirit is snuffed. Is it not worth more than skills and jobs?

In an externalized society there is less and less capacity to make contact with the internal, the real. Unless society produces people who can outgrow it by awakening their own potentials, society will remain at a loss.

PART III

THE

CHALLENGE

The memory of God comes to the quiet mind.
It cannot come where there is conflict,
for a mind at war against itself
remembers not eternal gentleness.

The means of war are not the means of peace,
and what the warlike would remember
is not love.

War is impossible
unless belief in victory is cherished.
Conflict within you must imply
that you believe
the ego has the power to be victorious. [1]

Why Has There Always Been War in the World?

We can always find factors for war: industrial economy, border disputes, overpopulation, religion, and so forth. But it is imperative that we understand *why* there is war, *why* there is the energy of friction, *why* there is conflict within man. We are talking about some inherent part of man's nature that resorts to war, that makes it take place.

In order to comprehend why there has always been war, it is necessary to understand the nature of the planet and its different levels. Creation itself is beautiful. Yet as it gets more and more engrossed in the energy of the earth it becomes more and more aggressive and, therefore, isolated. In this earth energy, with its instinct for survival, there is fear and competition. The earth produces trees that compete for sunshine, certain creepers that take over everything. It produces animals that kill each other.

For the causes of war, then, rather than looking at individual incidents of war, we should observe the characteristics of earth energies themselves.

What the earth produces is competitive and wants to dominate. Competition is violence. Therefore, violence is inherent in the earth. That is the nature of the earth. And as long as man gets his body from the earth, inherent in that body is that quality of violence. As long as man's consciousness is consistent with the energies of the earth, he also produces those vibrations upon the earth. We can see how natural it is for armament to come into being. We have weapons that could destroy all of humanity and "might makes right."

Earth energies are violent by nature. We see it within ourselves: there is violence; there is jealousy; there is attachment; there is anger. What we know are earth energies with their cravings, wantings, and fears. Look at all the billboards, the ads, the movies, the media. See what is happening everywhere in the world—lives lived in a circus of activity. But can it be a substitute for reality?

What, then, is our function on the earth? We are to awaken to that which is not of the earth, to bring the Kingdom of God so that we can change the vibrations of the earth. The body is only the means of bringing the Kingdom of God to earth in order to transform the vibrations here. Without this transformation we remain part of earth energies, ruled by the body, inherent in which is violence.

Violence increases more and more because we are less in contact with our eternity. In this process, then, of isolation from reality, we use the energy of the earth. The impact of earth energies is strong on all of us. We know but the energy of friction for the most part. Ambition is the energy of friction. Anger and attachment are the energy of friction. Desire is the energy of friction.

We must change our whole concept of who we are. We cannot know peace through our three dimensional faculties; we have to outgrow them. The earth needs our peace. We came to this plane to affect the forces of the earth, not to get caught in the bondage of the body and time. We are the altar of God upon the earth. And we, whom the earth supports and sustains and nourishes, are not doing our job. We have an essential function and we are interfering by not bringing these other vibrations.

Earth energy always wants. Even in its giving it always wants. When we learn to give as we have received, that is when we will experience love for our brothers. Then we are part of wisdom and bring sanity to earth energy, freeing man from his cravings, his fears, his lusts and destructiveness.

Energy must express itself. What we express is a matter of decision. For us to remain indifferent is merely a statement that we have chosen to express earth energies which are warlike. Each person is responsible for war. Therefore, we cannot blame other people for we, too, are part of the energy of the earth. And as long as we live by earth energies wars are inevitable.

We have become children of earth forces—timebound and self-centered. Man, like bodybound animals and plants, has a tremendous urge for survival. And earth energies are now isolating us further and further. We have all but forgotten what relationship is. Now we have dependency. And at the level of dependence we have preferences, all limited to body sensations. Relationship has been replaced by our grouping together at the level of ideas such as communism, socialism, and nationalism.

Characteristically, earth energies thrive on friction. The earth is fragmented into countries and there are always border disputes. Friction comes when there is fragmentation. There can be no friction where there is whole-ness.

What causes fragmentation? What binds us to different social groups? Doubt. We doubt everything. First of all, we doubt ourselves. We do not believe we are loved by God or that He created us in His Image. We do not believe that Love is stronger than all else, that innocence is superior to educated ignorance.

Points of view do not relate with truth. Where there is doubt there is no truth; there is fear. Where there is anger there is no love. Yet any man who can turn his cheek has saved a whole nation. A man who cannot hurt another, who will not justify his anger or his hate, would bring an end to the arms race.

We see "In God We Trust" on every dollar bill. Do you think that a nation that trusted in God would trust in armament? We cannot have it both ways.

Where is the human being who stands taller than the stars and the sky because he is virtuous? His very being upon the planet is a blessing and a light.

It requires being responsible and honest. And we must begin with ourselves. We will soon discover how conditioned we are, how indoctrinated we are. Concepts, ideas, and fear are all earth-born. And all these external influences have molded us into a different way of thinking.

In the human being the destructive energy of the earth works through thought. All fear and insecurity are of thought. Thought knows nothing other than fragmentation. And in fragmentation are preferences, choices, projections, and desires—the diseases in which we are caught.

If we understood this we could no longer belong to any man-made dogma that further fragments. We would no longer depend on so-called social forces that fragment under the illusion of promoting harmony. They merely represent aggression. If there were harmony we would never belong to anything that is concerned with survival, for it would not be necessary.

There is a difference between humanity and society. Humanity, or humanism, relates with Eternal Laws. When we are part of society we relate with relative knowledge. Relative knowledge means that we can doubt one minute and believe the next; we can like this and dislike that. It is always relative. There is a constant struggle within and it is ever uncertain. It can become fanatic, but it cannot be certain of fact.

Society can be stimulated and led to embrace dogmas and belief systems. And we are caught in our nationalistic views, our religious prejudices. We have other people making decisions for us. The result is rather sad. We have become duty-bound because we are irresponsible about our own lives.

To observe this is not to react to it. Observation is not contaminated with a point of view. Real observation has no animosity, no judgment, no ill feelings. It just observes and is untouched by bias and judgment. Observation deals with fact. To be with the fact is to end conflict, and then harness its strength of non-duality. Opinions and judgment promote fanaticism at best, whereas the fact is something we experience when we are outside of duality.

A fact relates us to humanity. Fact cannot be taught. It is something one realizes. So then, how do we come into contact with a fact? Certainly not in schools, because there we simply acquire skills to make a living. Schooling serves our sense of insecurity, the sense of survival. It is a form of conformity.

What, then, is a fact?

A fact does not change. A fact is something that relates us with eternity, something outside of time. "In God We Trust" is a fact and applies to humanity; it deals with mankind all over the world and for every generation yet unborn.

Fact transforms a person who then steps out of the values of society and relates with eternal values. He is not against society, but a light in society. It is a transformation that takes place within. And then he contributes to all humanity, not just to society.

As Heaven's peace and joy intensify when you accept them as God's gift to you, so does the joy of your Creator grow when you accept His joy and peace as yours. True giving is creation. It extends the limitless to the unlimited, eternity to timelessness, and love unto itself. It adds to all that is complete already, not in simple terms of adding more, for that implies that it was less before. It adds by letting what cannot contain itself fulfill its aim of giving everything it has away, securing it forever for itself.

Today accept God's peace and joy as yours. Let Him complete Himself as He defines completion. You will understand that what completes Him must complete His Son as well. He cannot give through loss. No more can you. Receive His gift of joy and peace today, and He will thank you for your gift to Him. [1]

Deep within each person there abides that faith in himself even though it has been forgotten in the mania for progress. And the disease is spreading all over the world—more and more activity that robs us of our real nature.

The man at peace is the one who represents humanity. To him each person is a human being irrespective of skin color, irrespective even of his point of view. How little we know of what does not separate itself.

At the level of wisdom there is no fragmentation because there are no opposites. There is only One Life and the relationship within that Life of which we are all a part. Jesus said, "LOVE YOUR ENEMIES." [2] Mahatma Gandhi said, "The enemy is not always wrong." Unless we come to wholeness, where we have transcended earth energy, fragmentation and friction will not leave us alone.

What constitutes wisdom? Wisdom is the knowledge that you are blessed. Once you know that, your whole perspective changes and you represent God on earth. We are capable of loving all things, for all things are of God. Therefore, you are never touched by insecurity or fear or hate for another person, irrespective of what they do.

Wisdom relates with that which is of God's creation. It has something to give. Wisdom has the ability to act without the fear of consequences—you are your own person extending your own conviction, having your own feet on the ground. You are independent. Free—not of government—but of fear and vested interest within yourself. And you have a voice.

When the body starts to express wisdom, that body then knows serenity. When it is not expressing heavenly energy it is caught in its friction, fragmentation, worry, anxiety, the division of a "you" and a "me."

Our job is to see the friction and limitations of earth energy and come to an awareness that is independent of the earth, where you and I become extensions of Life, and there is no "you" or "me."

How many generations upon generations have been deceived. We are not making right use of the earth or of our bodies. We are abusing everything including our own selves. We cannot make right use of the body if we harbor ambition or fear. In the absence of a new awareness we remain what we are—self-centered and fascinated with accumulation and advantage.

See the tendencies of earth energies. They are craving, competitive, unfulfilled, ever wanting more. The body has choices; and those choices rule the body. When we are in the service of the body, we need jobs. Everyone is educated. For what? To work for those who have control over material existence and authority over people's lives. We are part of a mercenary society where we are drugged into jobs and sell our liberty for money, our energy sapped by routine work. Self-survival has become deeply ingrained and has become synonymous with jobs. But it does not invoke a yearning for the higher values of Life.

Do you not see the mediocrity of man so limited? What do we know beyond physicality and borrowed phraseology? If we lack wisdom, what will our values be?

Helpless people are easy to harness by those who live by advantage. Plants want to get to the sun, we want to get to the point of advantage. There is no love in it. Nations do the same thing.

If we understand the nature of earth energies we cannot condemn anyone, for we share the same characteristics of that level of existence. Yet we are far more than that. We are as God created us, unchanged by the changeable society that rules our body with its belief systems.

That is the tragic part, that we do not yearn to discover who we are—eternal beings. What good is all our education or religion if we have not discovered the reality of who we are? When we know only our physicality, we build a disastrous world.

Earth energies promote activity. Earth energy that knows only activity is devoid of wisdom. Without wisdom it destroys itself. And so each nation strives for superior weapons. Do you not see what mankind is doing? See how activity is spreading all over the world: faster, quicker, endless. Do you not see the nightmare of it? Where is serenity or peace? Activity has just added greater efficiency to destruction.

We then have to work in order to pay the rent, to buy food, to entertain ourselves in order to bear the routine of uncreative life. Distractions and violence are rampant. We do not recognize who we are; we know only what we have been shaped and molded and programmed to be.

What does our activity accomplish? More artificiality? More cans and litter on the streets? Deprived of happiness, which is within, we go for pleasure and abuse ourselves or someone else.

Wisdom is not of the earth. It is of Heaven and it puts an end to activity. At the activity level, there are always consequences. We can go on improving transportation, the media, manufacturing, and armament, but the fact remains that activity bears consequences because it cannot be still.

Accumulate this, destroy that. This is what the earth forces have wrought in man. For it is man who destroys; it is man who is the deadliest of all and the most primitive of creatures. Yet he is also the highest and the noblest.

We need desperately to produce men who are not of the earth. Christ said: "THAT WHICH IS BORN OF THE FLESH IS FLESH; AND THAT WHICH IS BORN OF THE SPIRIT IS SPIRIT."[3] Spirit is never contaminated. It is as pure as the Will of God. God created the spirit and the Son of God is spirit.

The minute we are identified with the body or with the earth or with the world of opinions, my body hates you and your body is suspicious of me; and I make money by having your body work for me. Earth energies are at work with all their cravings, wantings, projections; all their efficiency, technology, and wars.

We are primitive people well-dressed. We are traders and businessmen; we trade and sell our body energies. We are owned. What do you think we are going to produce? When we do not know happiness, out of sadness and fatigue and frustration, what are we going to do? What kind of world will we produce? Can you see the insensitivity with which we live? Who is happy?

Then there are men like Gandhi who can say that he would die but he would not kill. That is not the voice of earth energies.

Gandhi's stand must bring us to crisis, to the integrity to say, "I can no longer live this way." But where is the energy we need to come to crisis? We either submit to earth energies or we become helpless. Neither is appropriate. What is fitting is to see the fact of it.

Seeing the fact makes it unbearable to live contrary to what our real nature is. Our real nature is not of the earth because we are the Son of God. Even if we cannot understand this we must be determined to give all we have to finding out for ourselves, for we are miserable without knowing the truth of it.

Where is that passion for truth, for God—another purity, another vibration that does not have the physicality of compromise and failure? "THY WILL BE DONE ON EARTH, AS IT IS IN HEAVEN."[4] There is within each person the memory of God. God is that which precedes creation. Awareness is the light in which there is no separation and no form. In awareness we are much bigger than that which is manifest.

We have all compromised, and therefore, we have low opinions of ourselves. We find safety in withdrawing and are left with very little confidence. Confidence is born out of passion. This is not the passion of sexuality. Passion is not for things. Ambition is for things, for status, for lust. Passion has no opposite. It is a fire.

Our knowing only knows how to continue the aggressive, assertive, violent action of earth energies. Real knowing would mean that we are free of it. It would bring us to the energy of silence. We know either one or the other; there is no in-between.

We live by the energy of friction and are oblivious to what pure energy is. When we live by pure energy, who is going to dominate us and who is going to tell us what to do?

If we really saw that the only energy we know is that of friction, the truth of it would silence us. Silence is the pure energy we are speaking of, the energy that inspires us into a different state of gladness. That is the pristine energy —the purest.

Energies contained rise to wisdom. They have conquered unfulfillment and, in wisdom, man is free. Unfulfillment merely exploits earth energies and in that exploitation it murders or abuses anyone who stands in its way; everything is exploited and commercialized—be it man or nature.

We are still part of the earth energies when we are drawing attention to ourselves and want to impress other people; we are in the bondage of the self. Insecurity is part of earth energies. Insecure people invariably want to impress others, and thus they have a false livelihood and profession.

Begin to see what society does. The system has a routine and we no longer think love or truth are necessary. All we need is affiliation with the tribe. Nationalism becomes necessary—whether it be American, Russian, Chinese, Canadian, or Mexican.

Knowing this, we could not be taken over by nationalistic propaganda. Truth would keep us liberated from the influence of earth forces. We are protected when we know truth, for truth is not affected by earth energies. Our eternal holiness is unaffected by what is external to it. Our eternal holiness is what we need to extend; this is our original purpose. Something else begins to unfold when we see the whole rather than fragmentation. The unfolding of it takes place within us.

We can see the pattern of earth energies, how they work: greed enslaves us, worry preoccupies us; there is the law of punishment and reward. And out of these are born preferences and choices. We remain related to pressures and circumstances—what is favorable to me, what is unfavorable to me. There is no freedom in it. We begin to worship status and privileges: he is so and so because he has palaces or he owns a big corporation or he is a senator or he is a cook. Yet no human being is any less than another.

It is not so much what a person does; we must try to discover what a person is. The more blind we are to man's reality, the more we create an external world in which disharmony and the energy of friction predominate. How much money do you think nations are spending on friction? How much to keep it alive with daily propaganda?

Millions of lives could be destroyed by nuclear bombs. Have you ever thought that the root of it is that we live by the energy of friction, that this is what stimulates us rather than thoughts of peace?

Can we come to the energy of love that wants to share rather than to defend? Can we come to harmony rather than perpetuate the energy of friction? Why introduce the energy of friction into our lives?

It takes wisdom to recognize the situation. And that is probably the one thing we thought the affluent world could do without. Of course, we can do without it if we love destruction, especially self-destruction. The more earthy people are, the more violent. Earth energy is very prevalent where we create sophisticated weapons. Anywhere we are confined to the intellect, rather than related to ethics and nobleness, is a breeding ground for earth energies. Yet the New World is somehow aching to flower into new consciousness.

So, truth is necessary; love is necessary; something that is not of the earth is necessary. "THOU SHALT NOT KILL" becomes truly meaningful. "LOVE YE ONE ANOTHER" becomes a declaration of freedom from earth energies. Where everything is sheltered by the blessing of God, how can there be war?

The minute you are free of earth energies you are giving to the world something it has been waiting for. There is a relationship then. The earth provides the food and shelter, and you provide it with the truth, the light— different vibrations. Then you can never be insecure, for you have the earth as your friend. Seeking ends and the knowledge of love comes. There is love where there was fear. Your presence upon the planet has a powerful impact. It affects the very thought system of people all over the world.

Do you not see what an opportunity we have? Instead of bringing fear and hate and tension into the world, we can bless it. As a human being, as one who has that eternal holiness within, you have a responsibility. And the Will of God will help. Having heard this you owe it to yourself to bring a change in your life. All the potentials are within you to do so. You have already been helped by the recognition of the fact. Recognition of a truth takes no time.

We have accomplished everything in our lives through struggle and effort, by holding on and putting things under lock and key. It has seemed to take a long time because we were always going toward time. We have used time to deviate into, to wallow in with wishing and wanting. It is now very difficult for us to accept that something can be achieved without effort. But to end time we do not need time. This is the mercy of God.

It is our responsibility, our decision, to find out what our choices are all about. They are either based on fear or on love. There is no in-between. In love there is no separation between you and your brother. Somewhere you make a deliberate decision to love your brother more than yourself, and the interests of another become more important than your own.

No one can give what he has not received. It is only in the giving that we will receive, thereby establishing a new relationship, not with the earth, but with Heaven.

When we have love for one another, we are a strength to each other—a moral strength to overcome the energies of the earth. When man becomes selfless, bigger than his vested interest, he has something to give. Mother Teresa has something to give. To those who have the capacity to receive, the Given is always accessible. They outgrow jobs. They outgrow insecurity. They outgrow nationalism. They come to the beauty, the holiness, and the sacredness that is within them. To live a life according to Eternal Laws is to be awakened within.

So, do not look for wise people outside of yourself. Every single person has the potential. The Kingdom of timelessness is found within yourself. Having found it,

something else is upon the planet. That something else—
call it awareness—is not subject to the laws of the earth
with its fears and insecurity. Having outgrown everything
of survival and the accumulative process, your awareness
has no wishes or wantings. Fulfillment is the fruit of
desirelessness and the joy of having something to give.

And then the planet itself and everything upon it re-
ceives it too. You are a unique being and angels hover
around you.

Life is holy and so are we. We are children of love and
truth. We are part of eternity. Let us not limit ourselves to
earth energies.

Let us but go toward our eternity,
and all the forces of the universe
will be there to help us.

9

The New Age

There is a general feeling in this part of the world that we are in the midst of a "New Age" movement. We tend to think of "New Age" as something new, of today. Yet there has never been a time when there was not a new age. When man discovered fire, it was new; when he discovered the wheel, it was new; when he discovered electricity, it was also new.

More important than external discoveries is the inner discovery of one's relationship with oneself and with all that is. It is an internal relationship that bridges the gap of separation between man and nature, between man and man, between man and God. And the New Age is meant to bring a person to that inner unity.

Before we go any further it would be good to see how words have lost their meaning. It is difficult to communicate with people because everybody "knows." Today our very knowing—actually educated ignorance—has become our problem. We seldom hear what is being shared because we have already defined in our minds what is being communicated; we have our interpretation.

Listening is an act in which the mind comes to stillness for a moment. Something creative takes place that was unknown before—a new energy, a new clarity. The still small voice within is heard and when that takes place it is bigger than the self, though it takes place within the self. One such moment makes a person humble, makes one loving, makes one appreciate truth. When you discover that, you add a quality to your life and to the lives of others.

Who listens that way? Our excessive learning prevents listening, prevents the new; and in this way it has become detrimental. For external things, we need the senses and we need to learn. But somewhere there must come a time when the senses are stilled and another action takes place that brings discovery.

To me, this is the "New Age": the discovery within me that I am not separated from anything in the world. It ends dependence on external organizations, for it is a miracle that takes place within. And then relationship comes into being. In relationship there is no separation because it is an expression of the One Life.

Our knowing prevents relationship because we are unfulfilled, insecure, worshipful of ambition, and certain that "we" are going to do it. We can become very self-convinced. Yet it takes more than having a sincere motivation to make something work.

We have to question—not out of fear and not out of reaction—but to question with an honesty and a vitality that words alone cannot represent. This would bring us to overcoming all that is of thought. In the questioning is the introduction of humility. For the first time, *you* do not know.

In that moment there is an electric perception. Something else takes place. We establish a relationship with the Unknown, with what is boundless. It is accessible to all, whether it be Einstein, a great poet, a statesman, a housewife, you, or me. We change human consciousness every time we touch upon such clarity.

Let us call the "New Age" the living moment. Can we come to the living moment and its vitality, its wisdom and love, its care for people? In that living moment of the present we rise to the height of our being. And whatever we do has a blessing and sacredness to it. It begins to grow and it can know no failure.

The "New Age" that we know, however, is but a trend: people meditating, burning incense, going to health food stores, becoming healers, so forth. The trend will one day disappear because another trend will take its place.

Let us look at what the mind of the age is, for it is influenced by the current trends. Never on this planet has man been so fatigued and depleted. As a result, outlets have become of major importance. We must look at these things. In what way is our New Age bringing stillness and relaxation, not through drugs, but through some real inner comprehension of who one is?

Beingness is something of eternity. It does not get caught in circumstances. It does not do things to suit the trends. It is independent of it all and that is why it cannot be affected by anything external.

When we do something that is not creative, that is not an expression of our being, but only an expression of our ideas and our brain, life becomes dull. We then need beer, cigarettes, potato chips, cinemas, newspapers, and so forth.

When we talk about the world getting worse, we are saying that we cannot depend on the external world, that it is a sinking ship. If we know it is a sinking ship we do something about it. But the tendency is for us not to hear, or to hear and forget. Nothing lasts, no matter how big the commotion.

Out of all this commotion many young people get involved in sexuality and drugs. More destruction of morality. We cannot ignore that. In what way has the New Age movement brought about moral strength, the standing up for a principle by which one would live no matter what the circumstances?

It is each person's responsibility to find out whether there is any validity to moral strength. New Age leaders flourish where people have not given thought to it. But what is new about their own lives? Are new ethics more prevalent?

Jesus came and there was something new. He did not have a church; He did not hire labor to build one; and He never charged money. That was new. Have you known anyone like that? Then what is new?

Trends come and go. I would call "trends" the old age, not the new. The old is based on time, on "me and mine." And the new is to be related to eternity. That is its difference.

Trends have fascinated many people. At one point non-violence was introduced and many people participated in strikes based on human issues. Today, strikes are prevalent where labor unions bargain for profit, but hardly ever for some moral principle. What does that say to you? That people are complacent? That on moral issues we seldom take a stand?

The New Age can exist where there is respect for a person who stands for some ethic. It would require some sacrifice, some renunciation, some integrity. Where are the leaders today who live by these?

Let us, for instance, look at the recent history of India. The freedom of India came, due to Gandhi and many thousands of other men who had gone to prison because they stood for some conviction, some idea for which they could sacrifice everything—men of ethics and integrity. They had some moral principle by which they lived, some standard. They discovered the principle of non-violence and brought that to application. That was new. Tolstoy had spoken of it; Ruskin had spoken of it; Thoreau had spoken of it; as had the ancient scriptures. But it had not been brought to application at the collective level.

The freedom of India from Great Britain was achieved peacefully. This is quite a historical event because those who rule a nation do not necessarily want to leave when the situation is profitable. And those who revolt usually resort to some form of violence and war ensues as a result of "might is right."

And so, non-violence caught fire. It was felt to be a great contribution to all of mankind because now the way was being paved to settle issues through the means of non-violence. Throughout the world non-violence was spoken of as "new"—a New Age.

Where is non-violence today? There is more armament than mankind has ever known. Do governments listen to protests anymore? Where is the New Age and the betterment it was meant to bring? When the media controls people, we are made more helpless than ever. In that sense, I would say the degeneration—the decline in morality and ethics—is far greater.

Since the end of the Second World War, tension, insecurity, and fear have increased measurably, as has the propaganda against the "enemy." And that is the New Age?

Be aware! Belief in the New Age is more prevalent than the actuality of the New Age.

If the New Age were a fact, we would have greater freedom. There would be greater peace both in our lives and externally. Governments would not be spending so much money on armament and defense systems. We would have more leisure and would be waking up within, finding our own resources rather than becoming more dependent on stimulation, pleasure, and liquor. The increase in tension and outlets is more prominent today than ever. And then we become dependent on the indulgence that society promotes—all kinds of outlets so that we can escape from our own inner poverty.

It is necessary to have a broad view of the state of the world. We can see that there is a proliferation of armament, humanity is more controlled, we have a perverted value system, and real democracy is on the decline.

Today, the United States government is gripped by a tremendous deficit. Someone has to pay that debt. How did it come about if not through irresponsibility and lack of wisdom? Why would we allow a government to be under debt? And that is the New Age? Do you realize how many generations it will take to pay such a deficit? Can you see the consequences it is going to bring and how much suffering it is going to cause all of humanity? Do you think you are going to escape its consequences? Is this the New Age—people talking about betterment when the facts are otherwise?

How would you look at it if you were humanistic? How do you look at it as a citizen?

May we begin by just seeing the fact? Awaken yourself and find out. Where is most of the national income spent? On armament? Or does it go toward the human being, for his comfort, his betterment? Is there more concern about those who have less in the world? Are we beginning to function as one humanity or are we still with the opportunistic attitude that "me and mine" comes first, both at the national level and at the individual level? In this New Age, is "me and mine" any less dominant?

Within national boundaries we create these biased views and prejudices. But at the human level there is only the human being. Yet we have enough weapons to destroy the world many times over. And in the building of that kind of defense system we have become morally weak and corrupt for the most part. The danger to this country may well be the collapse from within the nation rather than the threat from outside forces.

We could say that there does seem to be progress from the standpoint of our scientific and technological achievements. But to what ends? What are they used for primarily? The finest scientists—what are they producing? Nuclear weapons? Missiles? Only a portion of their energy goes toward some need of humanity. When we put most of our energy into defense, the abuse of science is probably greatest. Has man not betrayed science?

What does education consist of in this New Age? Does it awaken in the student his greater potentials to be more humane? Or is it to prepare him to fit into a job, thereby stamping insecurity permanently on humanity?

Is money the most important factor in the New Age? Is this the New Age, where money and governments control the human being more than ever before; where man has all but lost the liberty of making his own decisions; where he has become duty-bound and irresponsible at the same time? We worship helplessness. And helplessness is drawn to its opposite: to power and to might.

What would bring about a transformation in us today? Do we have inner strength or would we stay true to the idea that we are helpless? Could we stand on our own conviction? It is time we found our own strength—the love within for our fellow man.

This look at the status quo is not criticism. It is just a fact. Anything that is independent of one's opinions, preferences, choices, advantages, and dogma, must be very strong, very clear. It must emerge out of certainty that is not shallow or biased.

Fact gives one courage, conviction, a daring quality that is never in revolt or reaction against the external. It has love to extend. And the peace you find becomes the peace of all humanity.

Do not deny it; do not accept it. You have the responsibility to see for yourself if it is a fact. There is the idea which is fictitious, and there is the fact. The wise deals with the fact and not the idea because ideas are abstract. Evasion into something abstract is never new. The new deals with the issue here and now. When you have stopped evading, then I would say that is something new.

To recognize the fact requires having the ears to hear. We must be responsible, for the external is only an extension of our own confusion and laziness. And things are getting worse and worse.

We may not be able to do anything about the government but we can be aware of what is not ethical. And then build our own lives. I call that "New Age"—whereby we take responsibility for our own lives, for our own ethics, for our own virtue.

How are we to step out of a society in which we are bound by insecurity, bound to a job and to routine? We need indulgences just to cope with ourselves. There are more divorces, more crimes, more narcotics. There is more hate in the world, and greater tension and fear. If we value fear and insecurity, we will also value war.

The system is so strong that man is practically required to resort to wrong means in order to cope with it. Right means will have a tough time. There is obstacle after obstacle.

A person who is earnest and serious is already disillusioned. There is eagerness for correction; he does not pretend to know or not know. He questions and wants to know directly, not through the influence of another. And he must question because the vitality is in the question itself. Through questioning, we can free ourselves from opinions, assumptions, beliefs, conclusions, and consequences.

Negative thought is the highest form of thinking because it negates what is false. It undoes what is unreal. Positive thinking, on the other hand, asserts its authority and tends to make one fanatic. You cannot put truth in an idea or in a concept. Truth is free. And it is free when it has seen things that are unreal as unreal.

When we are free, then I would say there is something new. The new is within us, for the peace of God is within man. That is why all religions have emphasized, "KNOW THYSELF."[1] People who have that purity are the ones with no unfulfillment. They have found something within themselves. Doing takes second place to Being.

Being transcends personality and introduces us to something unlimited. Anything, then, that deals with what is God-created has that boundlessness about it. It is like Mother Teresa saying, "It is not a belief but a necessity"; she has something that is necessary. Mother Teresa exists independent of any ideas of a New Age. She is not of time.

I am talking about what makes an ordinary man a king—where nothing external or of consequence frightens him. He gives expression to what is new in himself. This is what we have to discover. The heart of a king trembles before a man who wants nothing.

It is self-discovery, not efficiency, that leads to the new action. This action is founded on the need to express the truth and love within you, rather than ambition and motive. This is where transformation takes place, and nothing can defeat it.

We must relate with the vibration of this land: "In God We Trust" and "All Men Are Created Equal." This is what America stands for. It is a new world. It must prepare itself to come to new consciousness.

Each person has a responsibility to love another—to look upon his fellow man only as God created him—because he has discovered there is no difference between himself and his brother.

This responsibility is yours.
To accept that responsibility
will transform your life.

10

Dark Forces

As we look at life upon this planet, we see there is great beauty in the movement of it, in the continuity of it. There is some other wisdom, some other intelligence behind it that sustains us with food, air, water, night, and day. It provides both our eyes and the light. It is not we who created the eyelids, nor even the miracle of the knee. There is no end of wonder about things. We are inspired to discover that there is some other force, some other intelligence of which we are a part.

Yet in the midst of the beauty of the manifested world, we have all but forgotten our Source and we live in a world of darkness.

> You think you are the home of evil, darkness and sin. You think if anyone could see the truth about you he would be repelled, recoiling from you as if from a poisonous snake. You think if what is true about you were revealed to you, you would be struck with horror so intense that you would rush to death by your own hand, living on after seeing this being impossible.
>
> . . .Today we question this, not from the point of view of what you think, but from a very different

*reference point, from which such idle thoughts are
meaningless. These thoughts are not according to
God's Will. These weird beliefs He does not share
with you. This is enough to prove that they are
wrong, but you do not perceive that this is so.* [1]

What are the dark forces that keep hidden from us the
light and holiness that we are?

Dark forces can only be of one's own consciousness,
some hidden fears in the recesses of the mind. Having
forgotten the Name of God we have gotten caught in our
jealousies and pettiness; in the uncleanliness of worry and
selfishness; in the insecurity and non-forgiveness of attack
thoughts; in the authority of problems that rule our lives.
We have a cloud of dark forces that we project around us.
We no longer have the confidence that we can call upon
the memory of God that is within us.

See what has happened to mankind. For the most part
we are panic-stricken, worn out; we lack the strength of
character that could, for a split second, make a break-
through in the bondage of time that we are in. We are
dissipated and exhausted because there is so little virtue in
our lives. What else could we do but project dark forces
and be ruled by them?

When we are tense we want distractions, and we deny
the opportunity to give expression to who we really are.
We are forever giving expression to what we want to get
away from. We are always running away—from ourselves. We use our inventions to run away from who we
are. Stimulating experience is what we call progress: faster,
louder, more destructive, always getting away. Are not
dark forces at work within us?

Get to know yourself. Get to know how much loneliness rules you. Where there is loneliness, it has a partner named "fear." The two together have almost total control over us.

Fatigue and tension, too, are of dark forces, as are pressures and anxiety. We are no longer part of the rhythm of life, caught as we are in the grip of insecurity and worry. Anger, too, is planted in the brain of the man who is separated. It has deep roots. How would you uproot anger?

And in the midst of it we cannot recall the reality of who we really are. What could be worse?

We must wake up and see what we have done to our lives. Have we not become part of insanity and its destructiveness? Are not the dark forces stronger in our lives? Is there anything darker than the fear that constitutes insecurity?

And what do you think newspapers carry? Are they not the perpetuators of fear and violence and thus, promoters of dark forces? Do not be frightened of what dark forces are going to do. Just look at what they have already done and what they are doing now.

Each one of us is wrapped in our own survival. We are part of a very conditioned, centuries old, worn out brain, steeped in superstition and fear. Our thoughts emerge from this brain. What prevents us from being awakened from dark forces? The attractions and indulgence that make our lives so anxious and self-centered? Have we taken any interest in emptying ourselves of insecurity and problems, fear and unfulfillment? Why do we choose to live in the darkness of consequences? We are here to serve God, not expedience.

The situation demands that we come to a new strength, awakening different dimensions within ourselves and finding our greater potentials. If we are dependent on sensation we will never rise beyond it. Sensation is also part of dark forces. Try to step out of it and you will discover what hold it has. For us to survive upon the planet some of us must rise above sensation. Otherwise desire may well lead to the destruction of the world.

Only a few generations ago we had an ox for our plough, a horse for our carriage. Today it is the human being that is yoked to corporations. Dark forces are at work.

What we need to rise above sensation, the universities cannot impart. They merely provide skills for jobs—we are like beasts of burden. And so we have our jobs, our routines, our favorite outlets—the diversions and the distractions. It is called decadence, for it is self-destructive. There is no peace in it.

How rapidly we are losing the discrimination to see what is essential work and what is a mere job. Meaningful work is essential to a balanced life. Who but the few dare to overcome deeply ingrained insecurity, having found their own productive and meaningful work? Without fully understanding the work that balances life, idealism and realism cannot be reconciled.

Work is another name for realization, which means right livelihood, freedom from want, rightmindedness, and value. Realization frees us from external influences and makes us stand on our own, unafraid in the midst of a mercenary society.

To be self-reliant is the first step. Self-reliance is both a strength and a necessity. We think we understand it. Yet our intentions are but forms of wanting which we consider real. Thus, deception—an understanding that is not valid —continues its loveless existence and generates our present predicament.

Today, for the most part, we are more dull and more mediocre than ever before. That is the trend of decadence. It only leads us to more violence, more sensation, and more distractions in order to cope with our loneliness and boredom.

And where does all our energy go? Into self-destruction —on a national as well as individual level. Each person becomes an enemy to himself. That is certainly not the right use of God-given energy.

We have to wake up from this madness and insanity. It should concern each one of us that society is degenerating. You are an individual, a human being, created in the image of God. Will you not wake up from your slumber and indifference and recognize the holiness of your own life?

Our relationship with God is important, for it is real. And only those few who keep it intact leave upon the planet a voice that still vibrates and is alive. Without this, our relationships with one another—where jobs, money, and survival predominate—remain incomplete.

Discrimination is essential to know the false as the false. That which sees the false as the false is not the false.

This seeing is the light that surrounds you and is ever with you.

We can begin by questioning everything. We can question the authority of dark forces, the authority of what conditions us. It is important that we see fatigue, anxiety, insecurity, and unfulfillment for what they are.

No matter how long the journey is, it does not begin until we take the first step.

Our function is to dissolve the dark forces and bring light where there is darkness.

> *It is your forgiveness that will bring the world of darkness to the light. It is your forgiveness that lets you recognize the light in which you see. Forgiveness is the demonstration that you are the light of the world.* [2]

I am the light of the world[3] is real in us when we introduce forgiveness into our brain. Then there is no impurity, no animosity within the brain.

> *The purpose of the world you see is to obscure your function of forgiveness, and provide you with a justification for forgetting it. It is the temptation to abandon God and His Son by taking on a physical appearance. It is this the body's eyes look upon.* [4]

> *Your picture of the world can only mirror what is within. The source of neither light nor darkness can be found without. Grievances darken your mind, and you look out on a darkened world.*

> *Forgiveness lifts the darkness, reasserts your will,*
> *and lets you look upon a world of light.* [5]

When we have come to forgiveness, Heaven's light will be ours, given to us and through us to all of mankind. Forgiveness dispels all fear, tension, and anxiety, for its light cannot be contaminated.

Let us be the light of the world that we are, for God Himself is in our mind.

> *Who is the light of the world except God's Son?*
> *This, then, is merely a statement of the truth*
> *about yourself. It is the opposite of a statement of*
> *pride, of arrogance, or of self-deception. It does*
> *not describe the self concept you have made. It*
> *does not refer to any of the characteristics with*
> *which you have endowed your idols. It refers to*
> *you as you were created by God. It simply states*
> *the truth.*
>
> *. . . It is not humility to insist you cannot be the*
> *light of the world if that is the function God as-*
> *signed to you. . . . This is a beginning step in*
> *accepting your real function on earth.* [6]

To be the light of the world, then, is our function. It requires that we come to a deliberate decision to accept the attributes of God that we are. A deliberate decision is the action of the will. It brings a total renewal in one's whole being.

Either we trust in God, in the function He has given us, or we remain preoccupied with our own. This is the only decision. God's creation exists to bring man to his own holiness. God sees only perfection. This perfection, this light, has surrounded us from the beginning of time, even though we have been unaware of it.

When we are touched by the light of eternity, it introduces us to the love that is in our hearts. It is unlimited in its unfolding. One Buddha . . . and his light remains forever. It is always the One.

"I will there be light."

Today we are considering the will you share with God. This is not the same as the ego's idle wishes, out of which darkness and nothingness arise. The will you share with God has all the power of creation in it.

. . . the light that shines upon this world reflects your will, and so it must be in you that we will look for it. [7]

This is where we will find it, within ourselves. Therefore, we are most blessed.

True light is strength, and strength is sinlessness. If you remain as God created you, you must be strong and light must be in you. He Who ensured your sinlessness must be the guarantee of strength and light as well. You are as God created you. Darkness cannot obscure the glory of God's Son. You stand in light, strong in the sinlessness in which you were created, and in which you will remain throughout eternity. [8]

Our determination and the strength given to us for our integrity and resolve would overcome the issues we impose and project and perceive.

> *It is God's strength in you that is the light in which you see. . . . His strength denies your weakness. It is your weakness that sees through the body's eyes, peering about in darkness to behold the likeness of itself. . . .*

> *In darkness you perceive a self that is not there. Strength is the truth about you; weakness is an idol falsely worshipped and adored that strength may be dispelled, and darkness rule where God appointed that there should be light.* [9]

We are more than personality. We are more than a body. We are of the spirit, created by God. The memory of God is inherent in each of us. Nothing can take it away.

> *The light of strength is constant, sure as love, forever glad to give itself away, because it cannot give but to itself. No one can ask in vain to share its sight, and none who enters its abode can leave without a miracle before his eyes, and strength and light abiding in his heart.* [10]

No matter what the external circumstances are, it is always possible to come to our own light and the radiance of our own holiness. This light is the light that does not see through physical eyes. It is the light of eternity, the light of all creation.

This light sees what is of God, and it is holy. It is a light untouched by time, not limited to space. And a few moments of it are worth all of one's life, for we are then the Son of God extending the light of Heaven.

We must have faith that we are a child of God, the extension of His Love. Our yearning to recognize this as truth would bring us to that clarity, to that light. We must not allow anything to interfere with that. And if we get distracted we need not blame ourselves. We just need to start over again.

> *Your sinlessness is guaranteed by God. Over and over this must be repeated, until it is accepted. It is true. Your sinlessness is guaranteed by God. Nothing can touch it, or change what God created as eternal. The self you made, evil and full of sin, is meaningless. Your sinlessness is guaranteed by God, and light and joy and peace abide in you.* [11]

Let us not hold negative thoughts about ourselves or another, for they are like dark clouds within us. By this means, we overcome the world.

The whole earth becomes a host to the child of God and pays homage to his presence that brings peace. All of nature longs, yearns, and waits for such a person. That person is you.

> *O my brothers, if you only knew the peace that will envelop you and hold you safe and pure and lovely in the Mind of God, you could but rush to meet Him where His altar is. Hallowed your name and His, for they are joined here in this holy*

place. Here He leans down to lift you up to Him, out of illusions into holiness; out of the world and to eternity; out of all fear and given back to love. [12]

The Forces
That Sway Humanity

To all but a few people the gradual decline in man's relationship with God, in man's relationship with man, and in man's relationship with nature is obvious. The word "democracy" no longer has the same meaning it had when it first found its voice. Religion, too, was to mean something totally different than what it now represents to the mass of humanity. Religion is no longer the actuality of a state of being where duality ends, where one harnesses the energy of Truth itself and comes to clarity. The same unrelatedness is true of economy and technology.

Interpretation is a major factor in this deterioration. It has little to do with reality because it is based on opinion and assumption. And where these are prevalent, there always lurks vested interest. Thus, selfish motives, ambition, and fragmentation continue to thrive. Is there not always one group or segment of society that benefits at the expense of another?

In what way has education or religion, economy or technology, or even politics—the forces that sway humanity—contributed to bringing the human being to precision, self-honesty, or freedom? What political system supports the brotherhood of man or the humanizing of existence on earth? Is not the loss of self-honesty greater than the so-called gain in expedience? Shortsighted views have nothing to do with truth or the understanding of reality. Prosperity and affluence, devoid of conviction, must inevitably collapse.

The people who are "civilized" are usually not productive in the real sense of the word, for they do not bring that which is of Heaven to earth. Their vision is not holy. They do not work with divine energies. Only the one who is co-creator is truly productive and civilized. The fragmented being promotes disharmony. Self-convinced, he exploits man with his horizontal values and beliefs. And under a myriad of disguises, man is misled.

Of what use is commercialized affluence to a man of wisdom and simplicity? The individual has so much to outgrow. Yet what is genuine in the individual is created in the image of God, and it is always with him.

In this civilization most human energy is drained for unessentials. The captive employees of corporations are cast aside in their old age without having come to their own self-sufficiency. They die hardly knowing anything of relationship.

The agony of separation, with its preoccupation with survival and constant need of gratification, is all most of us have known. Most people die knowing neither wholeness nor the peace that surpasses understanding.[1] There is hardly a face that is itself, or a voice that is direct or uncontaminated.

The industrial economy has assumed dominant importance and "jobs" have become as significant as Life itself.

Without a career one cannot survive in the system. From childhood we are trained to make a living, and insecurity has become the premise of modern existence. We are left with trained skills, not the certainty of direct knowing.

It is difficult for self-honesty to survive in present conditions. We are reduced to being a consumer. And with the advent of electronics that surpass human capabilities, unemployment is the inevitable challenge before mankind. This challenge, which is born out of a lack of ethics, cannot be resolved without virtue in the individual life.

A life of routine and compromises, inconsistent with our inner calling, must result in violence and disharmony. Internally we are poor in proportion to the externalized prosperity we seek. So much of wisdom and simplicity is lost. Human warmth and the hospitality of family life are all but gone.

What is man without divine leisure—the space a human being needs to know his own wholeness, the potentials of all levels of his being?

Society is caught in thought forms, belief systems, and bureaucracy. It cannot assimilate newness; and growth, if any, becomes external and horizontal and fails to elevate the spirit of man. This is the twelfth hour. Everywhere there is disillusionment and questioning. Faith in the Presidency is declining. Peace treaties and political alliances have little meaning beyond temporary convenience. Where are ethics and morality in a world that gives importance to pleasure, gratification, and power? Walk the streets and see the banks, insurance companies, and the cult of restlessness—not temples of the spirit, not shrines reflecting the vertical relationship of man with God.

Education and technology are seldom directed toward inner awakening or inner purity, nor toward the removal of deception. Even so-called reform in such a society is but reaction and change at the same level; hence, no change at all. It is merely a shift of emphasis, or more military sophistication and hardware, or a better way of computerizing the profiteering mind. It gives rise to more and more nationalism and conformity.

Outlets flourish to relieve the stress where life has become but a routine function. Confronted with a challenge, those with very little inner strength quickly fall back on habit patterns. One way or another the status quo continues in its helplessness, and the transformation of man becomes increasingly difficult.

In the absence of humanism, the compelling circumstances ahead of America will have their impact. Technology may well begin to fail. Education without morality will be ineffective. The economy is likely to decline.

The masses may even revert to the calling of "religion." It is irresistible in its appeal, especially under the present pressures. The call of "back to God and back to prayer," with all its tyranny of fanaticism, may duplicate in America the religious cry of Islam in the Middle East.

True religion, however, is not a dogma or a set of beliefs; it is a state of being that ends duality and alternatives. In it there can be no hate or revenge, no punishment or cruelty. Real religion is the state of Love. It excludes no one.

As long as unfulfillment and insecurity are not dealt with, however, we are compelled to externalize our life.

Ambition, fear, and selfishness become inevitable, making us inconsiderate of one another, and in the end, ourselves. Thus, we become self-destructive.

Even eating has become a perversion. The food we consume is increasingly artificial. The clothes we wear are mostly synthetic. Even the insensitivity of bleached hair is appalling. It is a preference for death rather than life.

Throughout history mankind has had faith in government, in prosperity, in religion, in education; these became the driving forces that swayed humanity. Man has changed from illiteracy to education, from poverty to prosperity, from primitive labor to sophisticated technology. But somehow we have come to an end in spite of the progress we have made. We have arrived at disillusionment. What we thought would solve our problems has not done so. The solution is not external.

Society will not change, but the individual can still rise to the height of his own being and relate with the reality within.

We have listened to goals and ideals that stimulated our self-interest: prosperity, equality, freedom, all the grandiose phraseology. How few, however, have evolved to find their own perfection in the living moment. Very few human beings have seen through their projected deceptions and saved themselves from the commotion of wasted lives.

Now one wonders if there is any learning through experience at all. Mr. J. Krishnamurti said, "Freedom is at the beginning, not at the end."[2] Wisdom avoids going through the experience of trial and error; it is awakened by the clarity within that sets one free from illusions and deceptions.

We have to heed the voice of vertical men such as Lao Tzu, Jefferson, Thoreau, and Gandhi, for they are not echoes of borrowed thoughts. How little have we heeded their clear voices, or the small voice within ourselves that leads us to the wisdom of simplicity.

We seek to solve problems and are taught to do so without realizing that there are no problems apart from the mind. What are problems? They are always related to fear and self-centeredness. And what is self but an abstraction manufactured by thought? Where is the clarity that dissolves all problems and the duality of thought itself?

To die to the self is the big fear. We have to have the courage of honesty and integrity to overcome fear, and then to die to all the conditioning and the illusions of the world. Then we will see there are no such things as problems.

Who has learned to end inner turmoil? The conflicting forces that sway humanity are all we know as long as we are subject to circumstances and consequences.

We have yet to learn to "TURN THE CHEEK."[3] What impact upon humanity such an action would have. What purity, this Christ-like action!

What, then, will end the sway of conflicting forces on humanity?

A point of non-deviation: the ending of separation from God. As long as there are alternatives to this, the shift and sway are inevitable and life remains personal, tribal in its approach, caught in choices and preferences, and caught in fragmentation.

When alternatives end we inherit the energy of Truth —the truth of Love. It is the Given made accessible to the receptive mind. And it is given to you to give.

CHAPTER

12

The Still Mind
Is Not Swayed

Perhaps the best way to begin is to present a fact. A fact exists in the Present. It is not abstract. The fact I would like to explore comes from the question: what is a "mandala"?

The first part of the word, "man," means, in Punjabi, the mind—the Mind of God. "Dala" is what you put into it. Because our mind becomes what we put into it, we are conscious only of the content of our mind. Thus, what we put into our mind is our responsibility. This is a fact. If we put anxiety, problems, and assumptions into our mind, then we become these. By so doing we have deviated and separated from the all-pervasive Mind of God. The duality in our experience appears because of this separation.

The Mind of God is a state of being—creative and energetic. It is a fact. In the state of the Mind of God, there is truth. Truth is never endangered.

Our mind—not to be confused with the physical brain —is part of the Mind of God. If we put fear into it, then we become fear and we extend fear. Fear is an idea, and like all ideas, abstract. We have mistaken the brain to be the Mind although it is only a storehouse of memory. It would require being alive to the clarity of the present moment to undo the bondage of our own little knowings, so easily threatened.

A Course in Miracles states,

> *Nothing real can be threatened.*
> *Nothing unreal exists.* [1]

Opinions are endangered. Assumptions are endangered. These are the things we put into the mandala, the wholeness of mind. Therefore, we must be careful not to put into it what is not of God, for if we do we isolate ourselves in our continual preoccupation with our personal dilemma. We must keep this mandala uncontaminated or we will not know we are an extension of God and that our minds are joined. We face a tremendous responsibility.

When personalized activity begins, the search begins, the struggle begins, the improvement courses begin, and we move further away from stillness, from our reality. There are no means to get there, for we are It.

We are so frightened of stillness. We think we need activity. And then we divide it into good or bad, right or wrong. We never seem to see the duality and conflict we initiate.

As we go beyond the right and wrong there is a space of clarity and truth where love is the only surety. It is beyond words. This stillness of the mind that is whole, so energetic in its intensity, is creative and productive in the real sense. The man who is whole is co-creator with God Himself.

The energy of stillness is the only thing in creation that is productive, for it is not personal. It affects the very atmosphere of the planet. Personal activity brings about war, hate, and fear. A still mind, at peace, is a benediction. It is a state in which we are not dependent on anything, not even learning.

The preoccupation of "learning" is a nuisance we must end. We have always been fascinated by it and self-convinced that we wanted to know and live by truth. But we used the preoccupation itself to actually evade what we were seeking. In this there is an inherent deception.

In the Mind of God, all search, all self-improvement, all learning ends in the discovery of the perfection that we are. From then on, whatever we do is an extension of that perfection. What we are is far superior to what we want to become.

We are caught in the idea of becoming. The personal mind—which in reality is the brain with its physical senses—becomes any idea it formulates. But awareness is never contaminated. The awakened mind never deviates into abstract thought. It dissolves it.

Ideas are dissolved in attention and we remain the Mind of God upon which nothing intrudes. Otherwise, we are in the bondage of ideas which make life at once abstract and personal; and we remain separated from the Reality that we are.

Awareness leads one to God's perspective. Thought never does. Thought is always a point of view. Awareness and its observation have the potential to dissolve ideas.

We assumed that to dissolve the idea and come to clarity required effort.

To dissolve all ideas and come to a wholeness, whereby nothing is outside of us, is to affect the very planet and the destiny of the stars. Wholeness has the purity of innocence and the space of the universe.

It is innocence that experiences the glory, the perfection, and the holiness of the Mind of God that we are. Nothing is outside of it—not even God.

Innocence is an attribute of humility, the most powerful thing in creation; it is untouched by fear. To that state every thought is external. Even the body is external. That state is religious.

Religion is a state of being, not a system of beliefs or dogma. It is not fragmented into Christianity or Buddhism, Hinduism or Islam. It suffers no division and encompasses all people. True religion is not a means of self-improvement. It sees that we are already perfect, as God made us.

There are many deceptions that we do not question. How many of us realize that nationalism is poisonous and produces war, and that only in the man-made world do we live and die?

Experience, time, and selfhood being our only reference points, we build a personal world of survival and success. Disappointment reoccurs repeatedly but no disillusion—the awakening within oneself. There is hardly anyone who encourages our rebirth out of cause and effect, the knowing that is not knowing at all. Yet we believe in our personal world without question; never knowing peace, we know only a life of reaction.

Can we begin to see the wrong premises upon which human society's belief system is based? Not much is done to encourage us to outgrow it, but much is done to encourage our pursuit of self-improvement so that we remain within the system.

In my younger days I was tempted to wallow in the ordeal of self-improvement and pursue my own projections of sitting in the Himalayas cross-legged—all the self-torture and penance that goes on with religious life. The tendency for activity is so strong in us. Curiosity assumes the importance of learning and gives us juicy preoccupations. We feel very holy punishing and denying ourselves. To come to clarity is to question these very thoughts, however.

The word religion also means "dialogue"—where two or more meet in His Name. Dialogue demands an intensity of interest that is not caught in concepts and does not promote one's own opinion. Thus, religion, too, is not a mere exchange of ideas or mutual agreement; its energy ends the separation between the two, the duality.

But throughout the ages, what has man reduced religion to! Behold the treatment of those whose lives expressed eternity: Christ is crucified, Joan of Arc is burned, Socrates poisoned.

Accused of corrupting the youth of Athens, Socrates said at his trial that the lawyers had not spoken a word of truth and yet they even had him convinced. This is how clever expressions can be where fear and disquietude rule. Socrates, the man of eternal voice, was sentenced to death.

According to Plato's account, a friend of Socrates later bribed his guards and made arrangements for his escape. He went to Socrates, urging him to make haste.

What do you think Socrates would say? The man of God who never deviates from the Mind of God, how would he respond? Would he personalize his situation and stray from the action of Life, or say something new that no man has ever said before, something original born out of the intensity of the Present?

The still mind is ever creative and productive. It is not subject to time. It has no preference in circumstances. It hears the Voice of the Universe.

Socrates said to the friend,

"It is never right to do a wrong or return a wrong or defend one's self against injury by retaliation. . . ."[2]

How beautiful! To know truth would require stillness. Stillness conquers fear and remains unaffected by anything external. It is an internal action within oneself which ends duality and brings consistency to all levels of one's being.

The still mind is undeceived. It is a state of fulfillment without which there is no integrity in life. Once you have that fulfillment, you can no longer be part of man-made religions or politics. You are out of it all. And your being affects everything that is. You love everyone because all are part of the Mind of God. Others may be doing things out of hate, but your love for the human being is not affected.

The planet needs our love. It needs the peace that we extend. Our reverence for plants, flowers, and animals is essential. We need to understand the stillness and glory of twilight that brings holiness into being. We need to understand the awakening energy of the dawn. Man is necessary on this planet in order to bring the Kingdom of God to earth. The planet is deprived of heavenly vibrations without him.

We are all part of the same life. There is no separation between "you" and "me." There is only the one Will of God we all share. Reality is what God extends; therefore, you and I are actually what God is—an extension of that state, that peace. This may well be the only thing we need to learn. But educated ignorance has not helped us to do so, any more than the natural ignorance we had when we were illiterate.

Today, you rarely meet anyone who lives outside of conditioned social patterns. There is no one totally free of them, liberated with a radiance of his own, like Jesus saying,

"LET THE DEAD BURY THEIR DEAD." [3]

Ours has been a tribal approach to a vast issue of life, with its resulting fragmentation. We are part of that tribal approach the minute we deviate from stillness, no matter who we are or what we are doing.

When I came to the United States I sensed a tremendous vitality. The unique vibrations of America began by integrating people of all nations and religions. As integration takes place, we move toward wholeness—allowing other people to be what they are, not relating with any belief system but with the fact that we are all part of the same life we all share. It is no longer a concept called brotherhood. It is the actuality of brotherhood, lived.

The still mind no longer has boundaries and no longer thinks that you are an enemy because you hold different belief systems. Beliefs separate us; the still mind encompasses all people. The still mind holds the world in its palm, caresses it, and blesses it.

Find your own stillness and you will discover the forces of that inwardness, of that wholeness, of that which is the Unknown. Lift the veil, and It is.

PART IV

A CALL

TO

SERVICE

The certain are perfectly calm,
because they are not in doubt.

They do not raise questions,
because nothing questionable enters their minds.
This holds them in perfect serenity,
because this is what they share,
knowing what they are. [1]

13

The Heart of Love

Sant Hari Singh, Vinoba Bhave, or Swami Vivekananda were not world-savers. Their interest was in knowing, "Who am I?" The "liberation" was liberation from the personality.

This awakened them to the light of discrimination. This single faculty of seeing the false as the false gave them the space and the resources of the Impersonal Life. In their contentment, they were whole. Having transcended duality, they set no goals, and had no ambition.

They responded to what Life brought them into contact with. The question is—What would Life bring to their attention? What is the common factor of separated man? SORROW. Sorrow is beneath everything we do. It is the source of all distractions. Whether one is rich or poor, young or old, man or woman, the dilemma at the level of time is exactly the same.

Great men and women, whether Mother Teresa, or Vivekananda, responded to the sorrow of man in its various forms and cruelties. Their lives are a response of love to mankind in misery. The function of love is to extend love.

If we take the example of Mother Teresa, we would learn that response is never planned. In an instant, the encounter with sorrow reveals itself to the heart of love.

Mother Teresa saw a dying woman, half eaten by the rats and ants, but she saw in the woman the light of her Divine Self. Picking her up became a sacred moment outside of time, in which the woman was made aware that love was upon the earth before she died. The action of compassion touches every heart, because minds are joined. Its eternity is not limited to time or place. That is the true nature of love.

The following few examples speak different languages of love. If we are inspired, then we have the opportunity of finding the potential within ourselves, for it is love that created us. The last example describes an action that is taking place with a group of people who are inspired by the Joseph Plan.

SANT HARI SINGH

While I was living in India as a young man, a saint resided not too far from my village. His name was Sant Hari Singh. Although he was a simple man and did not have a great following, he was well known in the region as a holy person.

Sant Hari Singh found his union with God through years of meditation, chastity, renunciation, and selflessness. He lived by faith and had the universe behind him. He was hardly ever a personality. To awareness, nothing is important except awareness, for in it, the psychological world of abstract thought is silenced.

For generations, people had talked about the need for a road to the Temple at Anand Pur, the Abode of Bliss, where hundreds of thousands of pilgrims go annually for a religious festival. Many streams flowed from the Himalayas and the dirt road was frequently flooded. In the winter the weather was especially unpredictable and conditions were hazardous for travelers on pilgrimage to the Temple. Although the Sikhs are known to be an enterprising people and the fellowship among them is renowned, no one could manage to implement the construction of the road to Anand Pur, a distance of approximately forty-five miles.

One day some of the leaders said, "Why don't we go and ask Sant Hari Singh. Let's urge him to inspire some action. What he says will be respected." To preach scriptures and talk about holiness is easy, but a true saint is a rare phenomenon. It takes discrimination to recognize the person who lives the Word.

A committee of well-to-do, elite Sikhs went to Sant Hari Singh. After a few minutes they told him about the need for the road. They thought it a disgrace that the Sikhs could not build a road for their convenience. If the government would not do it, the people should get together and build it themselves.

Sant Hari Singh was almost illiterate and he knew very little of these things, but they thought he could probably persuade a few people. Implied in their words was the notion that if he took action, this committee would back him up. They needed someone like the saint to focus the energy behind the project. The saint himself had no needs, for he was outside of worldliness.

Sant Hari Singh listened carefully to their plea and asked, "Do you think it is really a need?" "Oh yes sir." "Very well," he said. Because he listened, he must respond to the need. Now we are going to discover how a man of awakened intelligence responds. How does that awakened intelligence, which is always self-reliant, work?

For the saint the action starts with what is at hand. He doesn't know lack. He sees everything is a gift of God. Everything. So he asked the first person, "If you believe in this, what would you donate?" That sent shivers among the group. The man said, "Oh, certainly, I would like to donate; I wouldn't have come here otherwise. I will give five hundred." The saint said, "Five hundred? How much do you own?"

What a challenge! You can't lie to a saint. When he told the saint how much he had, Sant Hari Singh said with a shock, "You are telling me how important this road is, how desperately it is needed and you, who are so wealthy, are only going to give five hundred? Is this a joke?" The man was sorry he ever came. Now he had to donate a good deal more than he ever intended. The saint does not get taken over by the "idea" of road, he wants to know the actuality of their commitment. A rule of thumb was then established about the right proportion between one's assets and one's contribution to the project. He turned to the next person. "Sir, what would you donate to get the road built?"

He went from one person to the other. They couldn't leave, nor could they lie. Their intellectual, abstract activity had no love in it. Each one was compelled to give honesty to his words. That is the great gift of the saint. When all was finished, he had quite a fund to start building the road.

Sant Hari Singh's first action was to get the capital, the seed money. Observe how the awakening of new intelligence works. This inner awakening knows no calculation. It is simple, direct, uncomplicated. And it is extremely practical. It had nothing to start with and in less than an hour it has thousands.

Then the saint asked, "What is required to build a road?" It is good that he is innocent and doesn't know. He can find out. Implementation is easy once the resources are there. He found out that you need cement, gravel and mixed sand. And for the bridges, iron, steel, engineers, and surveyors were needed.

It occurred to the saint that in the villages there are huge kilns with the capacity to bake hundreds of thousands of bricks at a time from the native clay and so he asked, "Can't we use bricks to build the road?" The people said, "Oh yes, bricks are even better."

The saint traveled to the neighboring villages and told the elders there, "A committee came to tell me that a road is needed to Anand Pur. How do you feel about the need for a road to our holy place?" They said, "Yes, Santji, the road is definitely needed." He asked them, "Would you like to give your labor to bake the bricks for the road? You do not have money but could you give service?" They were delighted. Each village fired its kiln.

Sant Hari Singh made one important suggestion, however. He said that if two million bricks were needed for the road, they should bake twice as many. "Santji, why should we double the amount we need?" "Because we will sell the extra bricks and with that money, buy the cement and steel that are necessary for the bridges."

This intelligence of self-reliance is not based on business or economy, it is born out of love and service. Sant Hari Singh was not only building a road, he was awakening the people with his own inner awakening. He was demonstrating the way to do things. Everybody was amazed and the villagers were singing songs of the Lord while they worked. Thousands of people had volunteered to build the road.

The road from Namaskar to Kirtanpur was built and there were still extra bricks left over, as well as all the original money. With that they built a high school and a much larger temple to serve the greater number of people coming there now that the road was safe.

When I went to meet Sant Hari Singh, I didn't want to go empty-handed. I took a nice, woolen shawl which I put around him while he was sitting. The love of this saint transformed my life. I learned what it is to be yourself, what it is to be awakened from within, and how not to get lost in worldliness. The self-reliance he embodied sowed a seed in me.

Everything Sant Hari Singh is going to do is simple. He introduces us to a state that has no lack. It is joyous because the power of givingness is in it. Nothing can stand before the power of love. Nothing. The saint teaches us that the currencies of this intelligence are the power of love and the joy of service.

SWAMI VIVEKANANDA

Swami Vivekananda, a disciple of Sri Ramakrishna, came to America at the turn of the century to address the

World Parliament of Religions in Chicago. Nobel prize recipient, Romain Rolland, renowned wise man of Europe, had the following to say about him:

> "Vivekananda's words are great music, phrases in the style of Beethoven, stirring rhythms like the march of Handel choruses. I cannot touch these sayings of his, scattered as they are through the pages of books at thirty years' distance, without receiving a thrill through my body like an electric shock. And what shocks, what transports must have been produced when in burning words they issued from the lips of the hero!" [1]

The greatness of Swami Vivekananda is inexplainable, and yet an encounter between him and John D. Rockefeller goes far toward doing so. Swami Vivekananda was staying in Chicago at the home of a man who was an associate of Mr. Rockefeller. One day, Rockefeller went to visit him. The account of their meeting in the book, *Swami Vivekananda in the West: New Discoveries*, by Marie Louise Borke, says:

> "Swamiji told Rockefeller much of his past that was not known to any but himself, and made him understand that the money he had already accumulated was not his, that he was only a channel and that his duty was to do good to the world—that God had given him all his wealth in order that he might have an opportunity to help and do good to people.

> "Rockefeller was annoyed that anyone dared to talk to him that way and tell him what to do. He

left the room in irritation, not even saying good-bye. But about a week after, again without being announced, he entered Swamiji's study and, finding him the same as before, threw on his desk a paper which told of his plans to donate an enormous sum of money toward the financing of a public institution.

" 'Well, there you are,' he said. 'You must be satisfied now, and you can thank me for it.' Swami Vivekananda did not even lift his eyes, did not move. Then taking the paper, he quietly read it, saying: 'It is for you to thank me.' That was all. This was Rockefeller's first large donation to the public welfare.

. . . "Rockefeller . . . once, almost as though echoing Swamiji . . . said, explaining the reason behind his monumental philanthropies: 'There is more to life than the accumulation of money. Money is a trust in one's hands. To use it improperly is a great sin. The best way to prepare for the end of life is to live for others. That is what I am trying to do.' "[2]

Swami Vivekananda's true words gave life to Rockefeller. Honesty is the greatest service to mankind, for it lends itself to one's internal awakening. True words are seldom heard, but when they are, they can live on through what Rockefeller did and others after him. Vertical words are timeless and they expand and grow in the heart of humanity.

VINOBA BHAVE

Vinoba Bhave was a saintly person who spent most of his time in meditation and contemplation. To him God was the most important thing. When one man becomes part of God's Will something happens upon the planet. Vinoba Bhave started without a plan, without knowings or projections.

He had not spoken for many years when a small group of people came to him. They bowed to him and began describing their situation—that many people in India were hungry and destitute and had no one to turn to. This was at the time India had just gained her freedom and there were extreme shortages of food and other basic necessities.

Vinoba Bhave became interested as he listened, and the action was born when it moved him deeply to see the sorrow and the need. Being a wise person, he knew that changes are not immediate. He told them he would come with them to see their living conditions. After many years of silence, he made contact with a clarity within himself and changed his whole lifestyle.

The people were very glad that he would come to their small village. They asked if he would come by bus or train. "No, I will walk," he told them. "But our village is very far away," they said. He told them it did not matter, that he would see the conditions in other villages on the way.

That is how actions begin. One begins with an openness, not a mission. To learn, to witness, to observe, is direct. Vinoba Bhave walked through other villages and finally arrived at the appointed village where the people gathered under a tree. He looked at their eyes and saw the people were undernourished. As he looked around he saw there was nothing he could do. He was not the government or the landlord, and he had no resources of his own. He was just himself, one person, utterly out of his element.

However, helplessness and humility are two different things. Vinoba Bhave had humility. A man connected to God is never helpless. He responded to their misery with tears, and came to a moment of stillness. Something occurred in him and he asked, "Are there rich people in the village, too?" "Yes," they replied. "Are any of them here?" They said, "No." He asked someone to take him to the house of a rich man.

On the way to the house of the rich man Vinoba Bhave asked, "Does this man have children?" The person accompanying him said, "Yes, he's got five sons." They arrived and knocked at the door. The man came and looked at the saint with a white beard standing like John the Baptist. The saint said, "You have five sons. Consider you have six, and I've come to get my share." A new movement began. The man agreed.

In the first three years of his pilgrimage, Vinoba Bhave walked over ten thousand miles on foot, averaging ten miles a day. He never touched money nor would he allow others to touch it on his behalf. His own two feet were his only means of transport. Trains, cars and even ordinary bullock carts were out of the question, since money was at the root of their existence. He therefore vowed always to walk.

The walking saint had given up salt and every other spice in very early youth and lived solely on yogurt. At the age of twelve he took a vow of celibacy. He was known as a scholar, a great pundit in the literature of Marathi, his native tongue, and had taught himself fifteen other languages, in order to be able to communicate with the peoples of his land.

This humble person lived in a tent furnished only with a crisscross mattress of strings on a wooden bedstead, a few spinning wheels, and a pile of newspapers. Hallam Tennyson describes Vinoba Bhave thus, "[He] had an extraordinary grace, style and repose. The back was straight as a bamboo . . . The unwrinkled face—once you disentangle it from the beard—was completely ageless: it might have been that of a man of thirty or forty . . . Through it shone the eyes of a young man, gray-green and twinkling, as if impatient to break out of the mask becoming to a saint."[3]

Starting on foot in April of 1951, Vinoba Bhave persuaded the landlords of India to give one-sixth of their land for redistribution to the landless poor. By 1954 this movement had acquired nearly four million acres, an area larger than the state of Connecticut. It has probably tripled since then.

In the 1950s I heard Vinoba Bhave was in my district of Punjab. I went that very evening with a heavy blanket. He was conducting a prayer meeting, which he did every evening. I asked one of the attendants if I could see Vinobaji, as I had some questions. He told me to write them down on a piece of paper, and that I could see Vinobaji on the walk, which was to start at 2 A.M.

Two o'clock in the morning in the Punjab winter is cold. I shivered through my blanket. A group of about fifteen walked together with a single hurricane lantern. The moonlight was upon the earth. Everything was silent. All one could hear was the footsteps of the people in this vast, silver silence. A little later, the breeze stirred the dry leaves of shesham trees alongside the road. New sounds began to enter the silence, only to disappear as fast as they came.

I was called to the front. The two ladies in front of me had lived in Canada and were describing the impact of artificiality—the life of distractions and stimulation. When my turn came to speak, Vinobaji said, "You have lived abroad. What are your views?" I said, "Dawn is beautiful everywhere." Now the minds were silenced. He said to me, "Your questions are very interesting." As I recall, one was "What does it mean to Be?" Another was, "What is the origin of a problem, and how does one solve it?"

Vinoba Bhave was very amicable and friendly and we shared a mutual warmth. He appreciated the questions and enjoyed discussing, rather than answering them. But he was much more interested in who I was, what I did, where I lived, etc. There was leisure as we walked, passing by small villages, where people were waiting in reverence. He would stop for a few minutes. Nothing was rushed or harsh. The purity of the hour made everything holy. Silence is such a blessing.

When we reached the destination, he wanted me to assure him I would come again. We parted company at the end of the walk, where a large group waited for him. Daylight was entering the horizon, and he was surrounded.

Years later I met him again. He remembered me and we talked about how the gift of land from the rich to the poor was a noble act, but that what would increase the productivity of the land was water. This new wealth would begin to alleviate poverty.

At this time there was another equally selfless leader, highly respected and honored, whom Gandhi revered. Jayaprakash Narayan drew my attention. I thought it better to converse on this subject with J.P., who in turn would discuss it with Vinoba Bhave who, at this time, was under the siege of well-wishers. My dialogue with J.P. is recorded in the book, *Awakening a Child from Within*.*

Once Vinoba Bhave was gravely ill with malaria. His condition was critical and the people around him tried to persuade him to go to the hospital. He refused to leave the tiny village of Chandil where he had collapsed. "Do not people also die in the hospital?" he asked. President Prasad and Prime Minister Nehru pleaded with him to reconsider, and sent the secretary of the Congress to his bedside. After a week, he gave in and took some medicine. "I am putting my friends and well-wishers to anxiety and strain," he said. "To be stubborn in such circumstances is itself a form of pride."[4]

In this one incident the culture of ancient India is revealed. One is inspired by the impeccable spirit and sacredness in man. Nowhere in the world is the glory of selflessness and self-reliance so admired. I wonder if there is another country that could produce 48,000 leaders who would stand for a human cause, and go to prison without

*Note: *Awakening a Child from Within* by Tara Singh published by the Foundation for Life Action, 1991 (pages 303–313).

malice for the foreign oppressor. Honoring the spirit of non-violence, these leaders demanded a change in the policy, usually without ill-will for the ruling government.

Vinoba Bhave joined Gandhi in 1915 at the age of twenty and soon afterward, Gandhi had said of him, "He has come not like the others to be blessed, but to bless; not to receive but to give." Gandhi regarded him, although 25 years younger than himself, as a teacher rather than a pupil. He had chosen Vinoba Bhave as the first person to court arrest during the non-cooperation movement, when the Congress protested against British restrictions on free speech and free political assembly.

PAT KERR

Pat Kerr is a former flight attendant with British Airways. She was scheduled regularly on a route that took her to one of the world's most impoverished countries, Bangladesh. The conditions that she witnessed moved her to action. Rather than waiting for her next flight in the comfort of a hotel in Dhaka, she went to visit the local orphanage. She describes the joy she encountered with the lively and happy children in the midst of sickness, crumbling walls, and the odor of damp and mold.

She began to arrange for flight crews to visit the children, mending drains, patching and painting the building. What began as a one-day visit to an orphanage became a dream to build a children's village in the countryside away from the crowded and polluted city. In her very worthwhile book, *Down to Earth*,[5] she speaks of her experiences of the last ten years toward the realization of that dream.

She saw something that needed to be done, gave herself completely to it, and in an unassuming manner, drawing little attention to herself, saw it through. The project costs approximately $20,000 per month to run. This covers food, clothing, utilities, taxes, maintenance, salaries for nurses, teachers, vocational training instructors, and the management team. Pat Kerr herself has never taken a salary from the charity.

Most of the children entering the orphanage were sick and abandoned, homeless and destitute, but after receiving tender care and attention, and being treated as individuals, they became lively, bright-eyed children with a zest for life. When the children depart from the Sreepur village, they are educated, trained for jobs, and have experienced clean water, fresh food, and an understanding of the link between hygiene and good health.

The impact is of one person willing to respond to the need of another that was brought to her attention.[6]

FOUNDATION FOR LIFE ACTION/ AN EXPERIMENT IN SERVICE

Life is too vast, timeless, and whole for the brain to grasp. Whenever one has some glimpse of its sacredness, attention intensifies and brings us to silence. We have to silence our brains to go beyond the world of appearances; thought has to cease in order to be with what is ever-present and unchangeable—the Christ that the human being is. Until we make that contact our real work has not begun and, in one way or another, the issue of survival consumes our energy.

But when, with the Grace of God, something else is awakened within, you begin to care for everyone and everything you see. One gets a glimpse that in moments of wholeness there is not the separation. As you begin to undo fragmentation in yourself—the way in which the brain separates—another action commences of which you may not be fully conscious. When this awakening starts to dawn, you begin to value miracles, the involuntary Action of Life. The learning phase is over and the unlearning of everything that blocks contact with truth begins.

A new action was born in me with the advent of *A Course in Miracles*. This is the experiment at the Foundation for Life Action in Los Angeles, California, a school to train students to bring *A Course in Miracles* into application. Through our work, eternal principles have been discovered to serve mankind in times ahead. This experiment belongs to all generations. To the degree that it is impersonal, to the degree that it is wise, it needs to be known.

The work of the Foundation for Life Action began as I was directed by the Scribe of *A Course in Miracles*, Dr. Helen Schucman, to do workshops. But I had resistance to teaching because it was my conviction that I would not teach what I had learned from another.

Time went by, but the uncertainty that agonizes the mind was absent. It is a joy to have no plans of one's own and to be with the freedom of uncertainty. To pursue a projected goal, no matter how noble, is invariably self-centered and has its consequences.

Dr. Schucman *insisted* that I do workshops. And I was then awakened to a clarity within—ever impersonal—which directly understood: "Only by removing other peo-

ple's obstacles to True Knowledge will yours be removed."
It brought me to the awareness of the laws of the teaching-
learning relationship:

> *The course . . . emphasizes that to teach is to
> learn . . . It also emphasizes that teaching is a
> constant process . . .*[7] *In the teaching-learning
> situation, each one learns that giving and receiv-
> ing are the same.*[8]

I was told by Dr. Schucman, "Put away your false
modesty. You are a teacher in your own right."

When something is authentic, it is always one-to-one
with the serious few. And it is non-commercial. The focus
of attention is basic and an intimate atmosphere essential.
Like the dialogues of the Upanishads or of Socrates and
Plato, it allows for the sharing of something unknown.

Our action started in a small way. We insisted upon
self-reliance and the commandment Mr. Krishnamurti
gave to me: "Never take advantage of another." This
eliminated dependence on the externals, for we refused to
accept charity or ask for donations, and directed our energies toward finding the treasure within ourselves.

The small group that stayed on after the *One Year
Non-Commercialized Retreat: A Serious Study of A Course
in Miracles,*[9] held during 1983–1984, became part of the
Foundation for Life Action and the nucleus of the school
to train students to bring the *Course* into application.

A clairvoyant said of the One Year Retreat: "It is a
process of inner selection, one of the golden opportunities
on the planet. But who is ready? It has to be an inner

calling, for that is the level at which the transformation will take place." Dr. Elisabeth Kübler-Ross, the physician known for her work on death and dying, said: "Those who emerge from the One Year Retreat will be self-reliant and dependable in crisis and catastrophe."

Self-reliance requires productive and intrinsic work. To come to self-reliance the students of the One Year Retreat began transcribing tapes of the sessions. They felt that what had helped them could also help others; and so they made the material available in books and audiotapes.

During a trip to England in 1988, I was directed internally to bring the hearts of all my blood relatives to gladness. I was being introduced to the action of completion in order to merit a motiveless life free of consequences. While in London, the Joseph Plan was intimated to me.

Joseph, a prophet of God in the Old Testament, [10] prepared the Pharaoh in Egypt for the seven lean years. The story is given in the Bible so that we may learn to be responsible as this pattern repeats itself throughout the centuries.

> *Time Magazine* reported:
> "In Biblical times, a famed Pharaoh once dreamed of seven fat years of plenty followed by seven lean years of want. With the United States economy in the seventh year of a record peace time expansion, signs are multiplying that for many Americans, the fat times are coming to an end. At the moment, no Joseph is available to persuade Washington to adopt frugal habits, even when the fat years are in danger of turning to lean ones." [11]

Joseph was a man who knew nothing of greed or fear. He extended who he was as God created him. In his wholeness, he intensified all men for all time. Such is Joseph, the prophet of God. This unseparated, eternal man inspired me with his pure abundance. In his stillness there was no opposite. Joseph was wholly himself. He always acted out of awareness. In truth, Joseph represents a state of celibacy, a life free of karma.

Spontaneously, his goodness and his sense of wholeness focused the rays of the Kingdom on earth. Yet in the world of time, this man of Divine Intelligence was falsely accused and cast into prison. Joseph had no revenge, no reaction. His honesty set him free to do God's Will. From Joseph we can learn that in the acceptance of Divine Will, man's life becomes selfless and impersonal.

The Pharaoh, whose dream Joseph interpreted, was a noble and farsighted king—one to whom the human being was important, not politics. Egypt's pharaohs, in their uninterrupted space, built the enduring and mysterious pyramids. It is likely that within the pyramid are held man's innermost vibrations which transcend the manifested world of appearances.

The Pharaoh had the discrimination of a true ruler and, in his heart, the kindness of a king for his people. His trust and courage made him an eternal king in the memory of men for all time. When the Pharaoh first met Joseph, there stood before him a man who had never told a lie. The Pharaoh, attentive yet serene, recognized Joseph from the strength of his certainty, which effortlessly extended the power of the Will. Stop for a moment and imagine: What must have Joseph's voice been like?

Intensity of silence surrounded him. The Pharaoh saw that one who lives by Eternal Laws is a law unto himself.

Hearing Joseph's true words, the Pharaoh placed no conditions. He knew that a law does not compromise. Joseph had something to give and the wise Pharaoh responded with giving as well. That is the meeting-ground of togetherness.

We need to know that true words leave their light behind for all generations to come. Thus what has once occurred need never victimize us again. Joseph's incorruptibility is now our strength. One's own attention is all-wise and ever-resourceful. We can learn from Joseph and the Pharaoh how to prepare and how to relate with Universal Forces.

There is never lack in the wholeness of creation. Thus, the issue is always one of internal correction. Deprivation and scarcity are misperceptions; they are self-imposed.

We must heed the example of the Pharaoh of generous heart and trust in goodness, who avoided the crisis by recognizing a man of awakened intelligence and impersonal life. The Pharaoh demonstrated that for both the state and the individual, transformation is possible.

In reading about Joseph, I was charged. It was not enthusiasm, nor anything necessarily mental. The direction was given. In my case it started in 1989 with the offering of a Forty Day Retreat in New Mexico. Over one hundred and ten participants attended. In addition, many other shorter retreats were subsequently offered around the country. The income from all of these retreats has been put aside for the Joseph Plan. It is entrusted to be used to meet the primary needs of mankind.

It is more than a joy to keep the Joseph Plan impeccable. What a blessing to know that ordinary people can be purified by the work they do when the Grace of God accompanies it. Nothing is as precious as selflessness that slowly purifies one's mind and spirit with the boon of service. I can truthfully say it is not I who is selfless. Selflessness is beyond the realm of words. But the Grace of God is miraculous. It can make the lame walk and the blind see. What is at work in all of this is the energy of Gratefulness.

Looking back, it is marvelous how Life prepared us with having our own intrinsic work; being detached and owning no property; and discovering the strength of rightness inherent in self-reliance. Until you have found your own voice, your own dignity, it is not possible to merit service. Now we are blessed with the sacredness of the Joseph Plan, which is the fulfillment of having something to give. When what you give is the Given, you are an extension of the Joseph Plan.

Joseph, the servant of God, lives by faith for he knows that whatever anyone does externally is not of God. The external can put you in prison, but it cannot disturb your peace.

As long as we live by thought, nothing we say is true. Everyone wants to do good but that good may not be sensitive. Good is Absolute; it is not of personality. The Goodness of God sensitizes you to another person's need and it is your joy to meet it. When you care, you heed another's words so intensely that your own interpretation and opinion are silenced. Then you qualify to be the blessed servant of God. Just by listening, you will know what to do and what to impart. To be the blessed servant is to know certainty. You receive what the other needs and bring light into confusion and darkness. In the world of insight there is the pure healing because you are not opposing the Will of God.

The blessed servant of God must live by Universal Laws. That is his preparation. Cleansed of relative knowledge, he purifies his speech and masters communication. He is ever aware of the Divine Action in his life. Order is needed to have the space and capacity to maintain the light that surrounds him.

Swami Brahmananda, one of Sri Ramakrishna's foremost disciples, said that one becomes truly entitled to work only after God-realization. He shared that in the joy of samadhi, [12] the world vanishes, and that peace comes by loving God and having true faith in Him. The one who is calculating would be lost.

Today we will receive instead of plan,
that we may give instead of organize. [13]

Our experiment is not only to outgrow organization but also to bring fruit to the altar. [14] The servants of God need the energy of love in order to receive. They will go out in this chaotic world, having established this capacity to receive, and then it will be their own direct light and extension. The servants will be blessed with faith. They could be in the midst of earthquakes and fire and nothing will touch them.

Five or six years ago, I had an intimation that our work would one day become linked with that of Mother Teresa. It was a clear realization at a different level of being. It is interesting to see how long it takes for something to manifest and become implemented at this level.

The more one leaves it alone, the more impersonal it is and, therefore, the more sacred. That is the way it is meant to be. This is easier said than done however. In one way or another, we always interfere.

When Charles Johnson and I traveled to India in 1989, we visited Mother Teresa's Missionary Sisters of Charity in Calcutta. The words on the altar of their little chapel, "I THIRST," [15] silenced me through and through. Mother Teresa was not well, so we met with Sister Priscilla who was in charge. She said to us, "We don't want money. We need people with hearts to give and lives to serve." At the time I told Sister Priscilla that I believed there were those among us in Los Angeles who would be interested. She recommended that we contact Sister Sylvia who was responsible for the missions in the western part of the United States.

A letter was sent to Sister Sylvia upon our returning to California. Shortly thereafter, Sister Angelina, the Superior of the Lynwood Mission near Los Angeles, called and shared with us ways in which volunteers could help. She also made it clear that although active involvement was not necessary, prayers would be appreciated.

The Sisters provide a home for unwed mothers in Lynwood, about thirty-five minutes from the Foundation. We began sending two people for several hours every Saturday. There were gardening, sewing, carpentry, and other miscellaneous tasks to do. Sometimes we helped in preparing grocery bags of donated food items for the needy. One of the Sisters told us that they had been praying for someone to help with the work just before we came to offer our services. They were grateful and acknowledged the Hand of the Lord in answering this prayer. Our blessing was in making the commitment to come on a regular basis.

When our volunteers return from the Mission, they are always inspired by the atmosphere there. It is most refreshing to see that there is no judgment on the Sisters' part regarding the unwed mothers. What these Sisters must have imbibed from Mother Teresa that allowed them to totally respond to what she herself had seen—the Light of the Christ in the human being. It takes nine or more years to go through the training. But just that one would take nine years to come to inner awakening and this sharing of life speaks of the quality of the Sisters. It is not impulsive. Not many people would last nine years unless their callings were authentic.

Our students, on returning from the Lynwood Mission, have remarked that it is as if their hands are blessed in doing the work. What a remarkable discovery, the blessing of service. You exist for your brother and, out of that love, you work. Our volunteers were also affected by the uncomplicated and unsentimental approach of the Sisters. It is obvious that they are about their "Father's business."[16] There is warmth and joy, but they do not have the space for idle conversation or gossip.

When we discovered that they often do not have enough food to give to the poor, we committed ourselves to donating fifty dollars a week for one year. We met as a group and discussed the value of being consistent in giving. We wanted to offer an amount that would allow others, too, to be a part of the program and receive the gift of being in contact with their work. The donation is used to purchase bulk food—hundred pound sacks of flour, beans, sugar, oats, powdered milk, etc.—to add to their limited food supply for weekly distribution to the poor.

We wrote to Mother Teresa in India thanking her for providing the inspiration and the means by which we could assist in the work of meeting basic needs of our brothers. Mother Teresa wrote:

> "Thank you for your warm letter and the kind sentiments you have expressed in it. How beautiful it is to know that you all have allowed your lives to be touched by the presence of Jesus in the poor. He keeps using the poor to draw us all together. In allowing us to serve them and in accepting our service, the poor draw the best out of us, or rather, it is Jesus using the poor, Who makes us the sunshine of His love and compassion with them.

> "In the measure we allow God to empty us of self and pride, we enable Him to fill us with His love so we may seek to give more than to receive, to serve rather than be served. Let us pray for all at the Foundation for Life Action that they may make the prayer of St. Francis their own and live it in seeking to love rather than to be loved.

> "The Fruit of Silence is Prayer.
> The Fruit of Prayer is Faith.
> The Fruit of Faith is Love.
> The Fruit of Love is Service.
> The Fruit of Service is Peace."

Dr. Helen Schucman, the Scribe of *A Course in Miracles*, had said to me: "Send the world your love. It will come back to you." Mother Teresa's work best exemplifies this statement. When I asked Dr. Schucman if there was anyone who really lived *A Course in Miracles* in our time, she replied that Mother Teresa was one. Mother Teresa is not distracted by the abstract world of ideas. Hers is the energy of love and compassion which knows no lack. She is always present with what she is doing, for her life and God's Will are not in contradiction.

After our students had gone to volunteer for more than a year, I visited with Sister Angelina at the Sister's home for unwed mothers. She said that our presence at their Mission was a strength and an inspiration to the Sisters. When I asked her whether there were other projects which we could support, she thought for a while and then said, "No, we have no needs." Now that is very simple.

Stop for a moment and consider what this means. They have no needs because they don't believe in the future. They know for certain that tomorrow will take care of itself and they have enough for today. It is a different language. When you really hear it, your conflict ends also. Their authenticity introduces you to a moment of wholeness.

We were blessed to become related with the Missionary Sisters of Charity in Lima, Peru, on my visit there in the fall of 1990. We were told by the Sisters that on many days there was a shortage of bread. When we wrote to Mother Teresa inquiring whether we could establish bakery facilities at the Lima Mission, she responded that she did not want her Sisters to get involved in a bakery.

In this statement one discovers the principles upon which her work is based. It is always related to an extension of the Will and compassion of God which provides. It is an action of faith and truth which only knows abundance. How inspiring this is. Mother Teresa and her Sisters have no sense of scarcity because they are the blessed servants of God. I wrote to Mother Teresa:

"... We see such wisdom in your not getting the Sisters involved in the organization of a bakery. Your love for poverty and simplicity is a strength and a guidance to us.

"We have been a witness to the work at the Mission here in Lynwood with which we have close contact. Our group goes and volunteers services once or twice a week regularly, and they come back beaming. We are also inspired by the work being done by the Sisters at Misioneras de la Caridad in Lima, Peru, and we are responding to some of the needs there with gladness in our hearts.

"We have what is called the Joseph Fund to meet the primary needs of man. It is to be kept impeccable, since it is entrusted by the Lord. We have dedicated two years to the service of the Joseph Plan and now there are substantial funds.

"What we would like to ask is that if any project in any of the Missions of Charity needs financial help, would you please let us know so that we may participate in it? We speak in an impersonal way; the funds are meant to meet the primary needs of man during the lean years.

"The Joseph Plan demands integrity and I pray daily, 'Lord, prevent me from making a mistake.' May your blessings and prayers be upon it."

Mother Teresa responded:

"I pray for you and for all at the Foundation for Life Action that you be God's Hands to serve the poor and His Heart to love the poorest of the Poor. Since God has already entrusted you with substantial funds set up a project yourselves so you may bring hope into the lives of those on the brink of despair through your service. Since you are interested in helping the poor, be fully involved in doing something concrete for them. I thank you for your kind interest in our works of love and for your thoughtful and generous offer.

God bless you,
Mother Teresa."

The Foundation has been a school to train students of *A Course in Miracles* to be productive and self-reliant, having something of their own to give. The Foundation was not to seek results, but to value what is intrinsic. Primarily, laws and principles have been shared with the students rather than concepts. Inner transformation is not possible at the level of mere teaching and learning of ideas and ideals.

Several years ago, we recognized that, ultimately, having one's own intrinsic work and not working for another were essential to be consistent with the lifestyle of *A Course in Miracles*. We have realized a life of service is intrinsic and free from the conflict of external thought pressures. The issue of self-survival limits one to the insecurity of personalized life.

Knowing that a motiveless life is free of consequences, the premise of the Foundation, from its very outset, has been not to be under obligation. People sent us money and offered us properties which we refused to accept because we did not feel a sense of lack. Our needs were always met. For us, the human being came first. We were determined never to expand the group beyond thirty students.

We have established a rapport with Mother Teresa's Missionary Sisters of Charity over the last four years. This has been most helpful. It is our dependability that has inspired closeness with the Sisters. They value our consistency.

The Foundation has provided years of one-to-one relationship, free of tuition, to prepare the students to realize that enthusiasm and sentimentality have little meaning in truth. Without dissolving the abstract and interpretations, it is not possible to be responsible for what you say or what you do.

The Sisters are a living example and their nine years of preparation have transformed their inner lives and related each one to the values of an eternal and selfless life. What the Sisters now extend is the natural goodness awakened within themselves. It is no longer work but an internal expression of their love for God.

Mother Teresa imparted Faith to her Sisters. When you have Faith, you lack nothing. The Sisters never seek, knowing fully well that God provides. They live consistent with what the Prophet Isaiah said, "Keep calm and be confident." Thus, they have the space within their minds to see the Light of God that shines in "the poorest of the poor." The application of Truth in their lives brings to our attention the joy of "LOVE YE ONE ANOTHER."

The Foundation has taken many steps to introduce our group to Mother Teresa's work and values. We sent students from the Foundation, two-by-two, to spend weekends or an extended period of a month in active participation with the Sisters at their Tijuana Mission. Each one has made contact with the actual experience of what constitutes service, or what is entailed in loving a brother more than oneself. It is challenging—the work of cleaning, scrubbing, washing people who are ill, nursing the abandoned, the poorest of the poor. But everyone at the Foundation has been eager to go, and they have come back inspired by having found some joy that was dormant within themselves.

At the end of November 1991, we were told that Mother Teresa was likely to visit the West Coast sometime in December. Because of the evolving closeness over the years with the volunteers from the Foundation, the Sisters invited us to join with them in making contact with her. Arrangements were made for the students committed to service to meet with Mother Teresa. And on December 13, 1991 the meeting took place in Tijuana.

Time stopped. There was no haste or pressure. It was a meeting of life with Life—spacious, and with moments of perfection in the Now. I presented *A Course in Miracles* to Mother Teresa and asked that she bless the seventeen students committed to service. She blessed each one.

The students are indebted to the Foundation for the preparation that has introduced them to a different way of life. Gratefulness is a power. Its spirit makes it possible for us to bring the external activity to an end without residue. We are all enriched for having witnessed the Hand of God in what we had undertaken to do and complete. During the ten years we never violated thoughtfulness; everyone has always been included in making decisions. Giving another the space for honesty is what made things work. This promoted a spirit of harmony and we have been blessed by it. The Foundation for Life Action has succeeded in providing different values, virtue, and ethics in life.

My instruction to each one at the Foundation has been: Be true to yourself. The One Mind of the group will attract Universal Forces to you because of your dedication to service. Those who have given their lives to *removing the blocks to the awareness of Love's presence* [17] will be energized and protected by Divine Laws.

> *God indeed can be reached directly, for there is no distance between Him and His Son. His awareness is in everyone's memory, and His Word is written on everyone's heart. Yet this awareness and this memory can arise across the threshold of recognition only where all barriers to truth have been removed.* . . . *All the help you can accept will be provided, and not one need you have will not be met.* [18]

Our non-commercialized experiment to bring *A Course in Miracles* into application in each student's life is a statement to everyone that the Grace of God is the Source of life and that newness is accessible. The new must always be free of the projections of goals.

From the beginning, the Foundation for Life Action, rooted in the sharing of *A Course in Miracles*, has stayed with self-reliance. It endeavors to remain non-commercial, having something to give.

The Foundation's first expression was through weekend workshops, followed by ten-day retreats. These resulted in a forty-day residential retreat in 1981. *A Course in Miracles*, having 365 Lessons, one for each day of the year, finally led the Foundation to offer the first One Year Non-Commercialized Retreat in the history of the New World. The One Year has extended for over ten years.

The present students have discovered that the mania of personal wanting, with all its tribulation, can only be dissolved when one has realized the wisdom of giving. There is no peace in wanting. Joy is in the giving and moral strength lies in meeting the needs of another. Freedom from wanting comes naturally when one realizes all needs are met by Life's Divine Intelligence.

Now everyone in the group is determined not to work for another or become a mercenary. It is this conviction that leads one to the life of service. The students must evolve to stand on their own feet and give expression to the awakened goodness in themselves.

Life is Impersonal. Until one realizes the truth of this, the survival issue is not resolved. The personal cannot end anything; and its meaningless activity continues its involvement with the past. Ending is internal. It lets the joyous and the peaceful BE. The State of the Living Present reveals:

My mind is part of God's.
I am very holy. [19]

The next action emerging is the Joseph Plan, which is Impersonal. It remains to be seen how it will unfold. The Joseph Plan is endowed with substantial funds.

The student of *A Course in Miracles* could be a civilizing factor wherever he goes, and spontaneously responds in his own area to the need of another. The Joseph Plan will extend simultaneously in different places with the precept of *A Course in Miracles:*

To have, give all to all. [20]

What is God's belongs to everyone,
and is his due. [21]

The Holy Spirit communicates only what each one can give to all. He never takes anything back, because He wants you to keep it. Therefore, His teaching begins with the lesson:

To have, give all to all.

This is a very preliminary step, and the only one you must take for yourself. It is not even necessary that you complete the step yourself, but it is necessary that you turn in that direction. Having chosen to go that way, you place yourself in charge of the journey, where you and only you must remain. This step may appear to exacerbate conflict rather than resolve it, because it is the beginning step in reversing your perception and turning it right-side up. This conflicts with the upside-down perception you have not yet abandoned, or the change in direction would not have been necessary. Some remain at this step for a

*long time, experiencing very acute conflict. At
this point they may try to accept the conflict,
rather than take the next step towards its resolution. Having taken the first step, however, they
will be helped. Once they have chosen what they
cannot complete alone, they are no longer
alone.* [22]

14

The Joseph Plan

THE RESOURCES OF MOTIVELESS LIFE

The Foundation for Life Action originated out of self-reliance. We did not have any capital to begin with. What we did have was the potential of internal self-reliance, with the power of its own conviction. We began with just what was there, committed to not taking advantage of another, not accepting charity, not asking for donations, and not owning property. And even though we did not have the money to pay next month's rent, we started with a feast.

Self-reliance is a state that precedes the external world of images, owning, and wantings. Therefore, we did not have any sense of lack and could express and extend the strength of rightness.

The first action of insight is to instantly end duality, so we never felt the situation should be any different than the way it was. Over twelve years, we never missed paying the rent, telephone, or other bills, and never missed a meal. And now we have the external self-reliance to give to the world and the awakening of the internal self-reliance to share with those who participate in the Joseph Plan.

The Impersonal Action of God's plan for salvation continues. And, without our ever doing anything, in some part of our being, we are affected and changed by it. Our values are not the same, and we are happier than we have ever been.

Fear and insecurity do not manipulate us. We are blessed by the Unknown. The more we become aware of It, the closer we come to having to give rather than to want. In a silent way, as quiet as the dew at dawn, the Unknown is cleansing us.

The possibility of inner transformation is within reach of everyone. Self-reliance would open the prison door for mankind everywhere locked in dogma, belief, and misperceptions.

Fulfillment is internal; it is a state of being. How can selfishness ever be self-reliant? Someone recently said to me that if she made one million dollars in her business, she would be self-reliant. What an illusion: self-reliance precedes the wrong-mindedness of thought. Nor is it regulated by the external; it affects the external. One man's self-reliance is the wealth of mankind. The business-minded will never know the virtue of rightness.

The compassion of God is in holy relationship. The whole becomes One, if one is listening with full attention. When lived, self-reliance introduces man to the abundance of the spirit. The intellectual or personalized life can only know scarcity.

I did not have a consciousness of lack when I was instructed to do *A Course in Miracles* workshops. It was not meant to be done for my own survival; it was meant to share the truth of the *Course*. Selfless life is based on knowing no lack. Being rich or poor is not the issue. The resources of selfless action are far greater than any amount of money.

The experiment of self-reliance at the Foundation has world significance. To the spirit of having something of one's own to give, the human being comes first. After twelve years of consistency, we are getting closer to holy relationship.

Self-reliance is a gift to the future of mankind. It is tested, and it works. We are to be self-reliant through and through to merit being with the spirit of the Joseph Plan. With the Joseph Plan we are entering the age of goodness. Gratefulness is the key. It is the ministry of the Foundation for Life Action that initiated the Joseph Plan.

The premise of the Joseph Plan is holy relationship with the world. It is an expression of self-giving. The motiveless is sustained by life eternal. It is interesting to observe how wisdom corrects with the light of miracles. Man is the light of God upon the earth. As an extension of the Impersonal, he has the power to change the destiny of stars.

The Foundation that had virtually nothing except fulfillment when it began is feeding thousands of people today, and the Joseph Plan, having its own resources, has the capacity in a materialistic society to feed a good number of the people upon this planet. Once you are aware of the forces at work behind the scene, you are not concerned with big or small, failure or success. Divine Action is internal and not subject to circumstances. The Joseph Plan is the unchangeable in the world of changes.

We are becoming more and more aware of the Grace of God upon the work we do. Hence, not only is there more space for true productivity, but less anxiety and tension. We do not want to compromise, nor do we want to get lost in the activity, and lose the inner quiet.

The resources of rightness are overwhelming. The Joseph Plan has ample funds to start our own "concrete project" to purchase large quantities of food for the poor in need. We are considering giving up to 5,000 dollars worth of food to begin with, to each of the new emerging soup kitchens. Every penny of the proceeds from my retreats and book royalties provides a continual flow of funds to the Joseph Plan.

There is an awakening of Gratefulness among those associated with the Foundation throughout the United States and beyond. Over twelve years ago, I was directly instructed by the Scribe of *A Course in Miracles* to do workshops and retreats in different parts of America. Little did I know that the coordinators of these retreats all over the country would become the centers of feeding the poor in need in their areas. There are over a hundred coordinators with whom we have established a close, personal contact. We are now offering them free training at the Foundation to be part of the Joseph Plan in their areas.

A Course in Miracles originated in the New World. It is the first scripture in English, and the correction of man's thinking, too, begins here.

No matter what the external assessments are, the fire of goodness is in the heart of man. Disillusionment may introduce us to the potentials within us. We may yet heed the call to compassion. It is in America where *A Course in*

Miracles and the Joseph Plan originate. When goodness is awakened in you, it spreads everywhere.

THE JOSEPH PLAN IS A WAY OF LIFE

The Divine Action of the Joseph Plan for the Lean Years offers the potentials and resources of service as a way of life. In reality, it offers self-transformation. The glory of the Joseph Plan is that in its giving it imparts the sanity of love also.

Selflessness has its own vitality to share. It is related to Life Forces and has the capacity to receive in order to give. The Joseph Plan is Life's response to urgent need.

In the most affluent country, there are millions of people living in subhuman conditions on the streets and in slums. This is a cry we cannot ignore, a cry that awakens the spirit of Joseph within the one who has the ears to hear. Humanity is one. No one who is a part of the whole will suffer alone for long. Even though we may choose to evade responsibility, violence will still involve us all in the crisis eventually.

In truth, everything we do and know excludes us from the grace of the present moment; we are ever-projecting a future or resorting to the memory of the past. Only attention will free us from the illusion of lack.

Attention is the light that awakens one to reality. In truth, there is no ignorance or deprivation—there is only abundance. For we are of Spirit and not just bodies.

Attention and Spirit are synonymous.

Attention is total. It holds everything together and prevents division. Gratefulness is the radiant joy of life. No duality or conflict touches it. It is all pervasive.

To be aware of ever-present gratefulness, the awakening of attention is required. The Foundation will provide, free of tuition, the one-to-one teacher/student relationship to the genuine interest of the serious-minded student.

Service is supreme. It purifies and frees one from loneliness and depression. It is selflessness that makes one's life productive and honors one's existence.

> . . . (T)he Holy Spirit's first lesson was—
>
> "To have, give all to all."[1]

Joseph, the holy prophet of God, had the wisdom of Heaven behind him because he extended Eternal Laws at the time level. The wise is one who has learned the joy of giving.

It is all too easy to idealize, and to justify being controlled by the externals. The fact is, hunger haunts mankind in the ever-increasing slums of the world, and lovelessness remains preoccupied with its ambition. He who has the time for service is at peace. And out of that peace, he acts to share his goodness with those who *temporarily have less*.[2]

Those who live by preferences are externally controlled. Where there are choices there is confusion and internal disorder. We have to rise to a state of right-mindedness to extend the compassionate nature of Mother Earth with her flowing rivers blessed by rain.

Right-mindedness knows nothing of the duality of loss and gain, success and failure. Ever productive, it identifies only with the timeless laws that extend abundance through man.

The Joseph Plan offers each person the opportunity for service. Over the last four years, the students at the Foundation for Life Action have volunteered alongside Mother Teresa's Missionaries of Charity. The Sisters are unpressured because they have faith in service. They are clear because they do not calculate. It is hard to conceive how Mother Teresa could have inspired something deep within thousands of these Sisters. They are unworldly.

The simplicity and purity of their lives inspire people. The Sisters give more than food and shelter. Their relationship with the people is direct and factual. The Sisters are spacious—they have their own rhythm. They are dedicated people, and they are connected with the Spirit.

The Joseph Plan, too, is a way of life. It is an opportunity for students of *A Course in Miracles* to extend the spirit of the *Course*. When they do so, it is natural for them to be an extension of the Joseph Plan wherever there is need. Having to give is what enriches a person. Over twelve years, we have established relationships with thousands of students of *A Course in Miracles* and other friends throughout the country. The Joseph Plan starts with them, but it is not limited to them.

The goodness in the student responds. Where there is a need, there is the student to meet it. Your own authenticity and the love in your heart is all that is needed to start a center to feed the poor.

At the Foundation, we have discovered that compassion has tremendous resources. It heals the misperception that causes sorrow and deprivation.

The Sisters of Charity say prayers throughout the day. The student of *A Course in Miracles* can be faithful to the practice of its daily Lesson. Such a student is not alone. He has the universe behind him.

One begins to see the rightness of *A Course in Miracles* coming when it did, and starting here in America. It is a response to the wailing cry of those who suffer and are lonely, and those who yearn to make direct contact with their God-created Self. It is religion lived, and its church is in the heart of man.

The *Course* helps one correct misperceptions and offers new values and transformation. It is for the active person of the present-day world of skills and jobs. The practice of the daily Lesson trains the mind to make contact with the second Mind of which we are all a part in the Sonship of God.

The Joseph Plan is a non-commercialized action where each person expresses his own goodwill and purity of heart. In the centers to feed the poor, if other people are needed to do carpentry or provide another skill, they will be paid because we know no lack and will not take advantage of another.

The center that relates to Eternal Laws will not be subject to circumstances. What is needed is right relationship with the Holy Spirit.

Society has neglected the primary needs of mankind for food, shelter, and clothing. In the survival-oriented society of jobs, we are trained with skills to run the system. There is no longer the wisdom and capacity to respond adequately. This is partly because the proliferation of cosmetics, fashions, outlets, and indulgences by which self-centeredness is drugged and controlled takes money and time away from the human being. He is hardly aware of the sanity he has lost.

> *In the mad world outside you*
> *nothing can be shared*
> *but only substituted . . .* [3]

And yet it is out of this industrialized society that something can be done at the level of people-to-people. Governments have their own agenda of war, economy, politics, and so on. We are to bring the focus back to individuals who care for others in need. Though small, the people-to-people approach has the resources of rightness.

THE POINT FOUR PROGRAM
RETURNS TO AMERICA

The Joseph Plan introduces us to the American spirit of the Point Four Program in our own areas by having something to give and to share with the poor *who temporarily have less.* The original Point Four Program began after World War II, and expressed the sentiment of this country: "The only war America seeks is the war against illiteracy, poverty, and hunger." [4]

Point Four takes its name from the fourth position on recommendations of foreign policy to the Congress in the inaugural address of newly reelected president Harry S. Truman in January 1949.

"We must embark on a bold new program for making the benefits of our scientific advances and industrial progress available for the improvement and growth of underdeveloped areas. More than half the people in the world are living in conditions approaching misery.

"For the first time in history humanity possesses the knowledge and the skill to relieve the suffering of these people. I believe that we should make available to peace-loving peoples the benefits of our store of technical knowledge in order to help them realize their aspirations for a better life."[5]

"The Point Four Program urged international cooperation to teach self-help to poverty-stricken peoples through provision of technological knowledge and skills and through capital investment. A 1950 appropriation of $35 million introduced the U.S. outlays that reached $400 million by 1954—espousing economic and social development throughout the free countries of Asia, Africa, and Latin America. Point Four necessarily confronted age-old institutions, customs, and vested interests—yet progress appeared in agriculture, conservation, waterpower, technical skills, and installations."[6]

"American experts in many fields—technological, scientific, medical, educational—set up schools, hospitals, and clinics, taught farmers and small businessmen, built roads and harbors . . . Truman later called Point Four '. . . an adventurous idea such as had never been proposed by any country in the history of the world.' "[7]

World famous historian and author, Arnold Toynbee, said of the program: ". . . not the discovery of atomic energy but the solicitude of the world's most privileged people for its less privileged as vested in Truman's Point Four and the Marshall Plan . . . this will be remembered as the signal achievement of our age."[8]

When the Democrats returned to office in 1960, John F. Kennedy's Peace Corps became ". . . an elaboration of Truman's Point Four program that involved sending young American volunteers to underdeveloped parts of the world to furnish technical aid."[9]

The Point Four Program was to meet the primary needs of man everywhere. That is how it started and the wonderful goodwill surfaced. Then slowly the program became connected with militarism and the insanity began. The insanity was far greater than this little tender flower, the Point Four Program, and so it just withered away. It was an inspiring and good program, but how easily and totally forgotten. The fear of communism took over and it died a natural death because America was not so inclined to help any country which did not give it a military base or support its views.

The Point Four Program allocations were a very small fraction of the expenditure for the bases. So it became a mere gesture and died. As noble as the original Point Four Program was, and as great as the goodness of the people of the country, government and politics moved toward greater concentration of power in the hands of the few and became more and more anti-democratic.

From 1945 to 1986, the U.S. manufactured 60,000 nuclear warheads at a cost of $750 billion—or four warheads per day for forty years.

President Eisenhower said, "The cost of one modern heavy bomber is this: a modern brick school in more than thirty cities. It is two electric power plants, each serving a town of 60,000 population. It is two fine, fully equipped hospitals. It is some fifty miles of concrete highway."

Never in history has such destructive waste and expenditure been justified and it is leading to bankruptcy. That America has become the world's largest debtor nation is a fact. With the power of the present lobbying system, the government is not likely to change its mind.

The Joseph Plan wants to revive the original incentive of the finer spirit of America. And I maintain that spirit is still here. The new Point Four Program does not go to Third World countries; it is needed here as the economic situation worsens and unemployment grows.

The Point Four Program of the Joseph Plan is based on a people-to-people approach. It has its own moral strength for it is not a reaction. It opposes nothing, although it is fully aware. We must find the resources to change within ourselves, rather than expecting to correct the mighty system.

The power of goodwill will transform the situation. It has Divine Intelligence and other Forces behind it; it does not need government aid. The Point Four Program is not to have vested interests. It is not ambitious; it is humane.

WE START WHERE WE ARE
WITH WHAT WE HAVE.

There is need of MIRACLE CENTERS FOR DAILY BREAD. The intent of the Joseph Plan is to support small groups who have their own initiative and can stand on their own feet. What is needed is devotion, integrity, and the will to serve.

We are to keep the Joseph Plan incorruptible and watch out for self-deception. Otherwise, it will not work. We will see how difficult it is, because the relative thought system will make compromise attractive. Partial attention can never cope with inherent unwillingness. But the vision of right perspective in a moment outside duality comprehends:

> *Let me recognize my problems*
> *have been solved.* [10]

Everything that is authentic starts small. It starts with the few who have inner strength. The Joseph Plan will awaken us to gratefulness—the law of abundance. Each student of *A Course in Miracles* can be Joseph for a moment outside of time.

> *It will be given you to see*
> *your brother's worth,*
> *when all you want for him is peace.* [11]

Right where you are is where your function is fulfilled. We need only overcome the preoccupation of wanting situations to be different. Each day give a flower of your heart to the sad world, and remove the sorrow of man with your goodness. We need to know compassion at work to be with the peace of God. It is love that transforms life.

Activity makes life self-centered and abstract. In a world of activity, we need to stay with the Impersonal action.

All is provided. This we will discover. The action of the Joseph Plan begins wherever there are people who want to meet a need. They are not to be directed by anyone else and they do not need to raise money. They simply start with their own resources and goodwill. It may grow as other people come, but each group must find strength in its own self-reliance. If their hearts are pure it will flourish, and they will see the splendour of how Life provides.

THE JOSEPH PLAN OFFERS TRAINING

We foresee a myriad of small service centers all over the country. Each group can select one person to come to the Foundation for Life Action for a period of training. There will be no tuition charged. This training will introduce people to the schedule of work and prayer that is essential to a life of service.

We will also help them with administration—how to start, what steps are necessary to implement the project, and how to set up a meeting place. The one person out of each group who comes for training in turn goes back and shares with the others. That is the service the Foundation offers.

The Joseph Plan is not for the impulsive and enthusiastic who at every hitch get defeated and project problems.

True service has a life behind it. It is contact with the Christ within that responds to the Christ in others.

The Joseph Plan does not require an organization. What it needs is those who can say:

I am here only to be truly helpful. [12]

The wise one is self-reliant because he works with "what is," not with what "should be." Each group has to overcome its dependence on the external. Your own helpfulness will inspire many of the hungry and abandoned to be productive, too.

The Joseph Plan is decentralized and starts at the grassroots level. Each group is to find the resources in its own community. It is strictly a people-to-people plan. Service is never abstract or idealistic. When you see a need in your area and it is direct, you will be inspired by the compassion of your own potentials.

THE JOSEPH PLAN
GOES TO THE SOUP KITCHEN

There is great beauty in service, in generosity,
and in honesty of attention.

A soup kitchen is to have the atmosphere of a shrine, for here living humanity is being fed. Soup kitchens will work if we have no options. It is as simple as that. The minute we externalize it, we have gone astray. Homes for abandoned children or old people too will succeed, *when we truly will it to work*.

You could start a soup kitchen for those in need. Order is essential, and the soup kitchen would have to be well-managed and well-staffed to succeed. As the integrity of your group becomes established, you could ask restaurants to participate. For instance, a restaurant could feed ten people a day. And arrangements could be made to use the surplus food that goes wasted. Then you would be getting involved with the community and extending a spirit of gratefulness and hospitality.

One could call on people who live in the community surrounding the soup kitchen to volunteer some time for service. They could offer an hour a day, or a day each week, or they could take on the responsibility for particular errands.

Your center would work if you act out of care for the human being who temporarily has less. What a joy it is to be giving a blanket to someone who's cold, a hot meal to the hungry. And most precious of all is self-giving. Divine Forces work with and through those who have self-giving in their hearts.

THE ATMOSPHERE
OF THE SOUP KITCHEN

One of the most important things is the atmosphere of the soup kitchen. Fill it with an aesthetic sense of beauty, flowers, and joy, so that it is a place that awakens the spirit of man that is free of pressure, and offers the space of leisure. You need never be overwhelmed, but always calm and welcoming. It is your reverence for life that will purify the place.

Joseph's soup kitchen is where we start with quietude and invite the Presence; calming ourselves, slowing down, to move from another space of quiet. Quiet comes when we practice the daily Lesson of *A Course in Miracles* with a different spirit and evoke contact with the stillness of Creation.

In the soup kitchen, you make sure that everything is clean and impeccable. Clean walls, clean food, clean plates, clean tables, clean floors, the purity of stillness, and sometimes music. This gives it the space. As you invoke the Presence, bless the food, and feed the people who come, the peace of God is there. That is what a soup kitchen is to be like. Wisdom has its own simplicity.

The soup kitchen would be a place that offers serenity in the midst of a world of stimulation and pressures. It would be a place where holy songs are sung and the spirit of blessedness is present. The soup kitchen is to be a place of order in the world of disorder, where the peace of God is felt in the purity of silence.

What we are to represent in the soup kitchen nourishes the body, mind, and spirit. Could there be one place in a city or town that has that peace?

NON-COMMERCIAL ACTION
KNOWS NO LACK

At the Foundation we never charged tuition because we were never poor. It is a different principle, and it works. Now the Foundation will help to start many other centers because it has the right premise. It is a response to the need of a group who wants to start a soup kitchen, a shelter for unwed mothers, a home for the elderly, or a refuge for abandoned children.

We will share with the group what the potential of response is. We will try to bring them into contact with the fact that they will lack nothing.

Even if hundreds of people were to come to a soup kitchen, the mind that responds sees no problem. It is an innocent, pure, vibrantly alive mind whose thinking is of a different quality. This quality is what is necessary, and *A Course in Miracles* imparts it in every Lesson.

THE SOUP KITCHEN IS ALSO A SCHOOL

The Miracle Center of Daily Bread is also a school— for those who start it as well as those who come for sustenance and the warmth of hospitality. The Miracle Center of Daily Bread not only feeds the people, but offers training that restores dignity and opens the door to a new life of self-reliance through productivity. The school trains for and shares the spirit of gratefulness.

The soup kitchen is a school that brings a new order to the life of service. We deal with the whole and restore confidence in the one who is in need. It is a school for the awakening of aesthetic values, providing space in the world of pressures for the refinement and etiquette which represent the Spirit in life.

Those who come for sustenance can be students, too. There will be classes after meals in the management of the soup kitchen. We meet to learn what needs to be done, and what we from the Joseph Plan can contribute.

> *What is God's belongs to everyone,*
> *and is his due.* [13]

The resources of the planet that sustain life belong to everyone. In truth, there are no limitations. The Joseph Plan removes the walls of resistance. In times to come, most of the staff of the Joseph Plan will consist of those who came empty-handed to the soup kitchen. It will not only be our soup kitchen; it will belong to everyone who comes.

So our approach to the soup kitchen is different. The difference is in recognizing that while food is a necessity that sustains life at the physical level, that is not the only level of a human being. Our need for the inner awakening of awareness, too, is essential.

A PROJECT IN MY OWN BACKYARD

Right in my own backyard, so to speak, is a beginning endeavor inspired by the Joseph Plan. After the 1993 Easter Retreat in Lake Tahoe, California, several of the attendees who live in Ojai, California, met to explore what needs they could find in their small community. Looking around them, they discovered a number of Mexican immigrant families who depend on occasional work for their support.

The group started by approaching the men who stand on street corners waiting to be employed. One person who speaks Spanish asked, "Is there anything you need? We're wondering if there are people in the community who need help." They passed out coffee and burritos and the men began to light up. One of them said, "We are short on food and clothing."

Starting with clothing collected from their own closets and food they donated themselves, "The Bridge," as this group of eight people call themselves, now distributes rice, beans, fresh produce, and canned goods to an average of ten to fifteen families every other week. Among exchanges in broken Spanish or English and lots of smiles, used clothing is spread out on sheets and the women find what their families need. Children enjoy the popcorn or watermelon the volunteers bring to share with their neighbors.

Two people from the group teach at the Krishnamurti School in Ojai, where one of the parents started a weekly sharing program. Students bring canned goods or other practical items from home and are happy to know the food is given directly to those in need.

"The Bridge" has also found work for some of these people in their homes, ironing and sewing buttons on dresses for a local manufacturer of organic clothing. The company pays them the same salaries their own employees receive.

I attended one of this group's meetings and was very moved by the spirit behind their project. It was a joy to see the purity of spontaneous response gathering strength in a single meeting. It brought to everyone's face a glow of kindness. Over the months I have seen it grow in zest and joy. They have even gathered large pieces of furniture to give, and one of the boys put together a bicycle to offer as transportation.

I am deeply affected by the goodwill in people. One family said, "We must give new clothes, not just leftovers." There is such dignity in their generosity. A young lady comes consistently from Santa Barbara, 35 miles away, taking time off from her own work. You don't have to persuade people; something in them leaps at the sound of service. What it does to one to see people's response— it inspires faith in the goodness of man. How can there be any lack when such sympathy comes alive?

LOVE CAN OPEN PRISON DOORS— THE JOSEPH PLAN IN ACTION

I met Starr Daily at Koinonea Foundation in Maryland in the fifties. He told me that he had had some religious experiences. There was a sincerity in his appearance and in his voice. He was not determined to convert; he had space. We were together for a few days at a conference.

He told me that he had been in prison quite a number of times, but the last time he was in jail, he was kept in a special cell where his bad behavior had led him. Prior to that at other prisons, he could always figure out ways, manipulate, and feel confident in finding a way out. But now in the cell, suddenly he lost all hope. Admitting his guilt and feeling very depressed, he was compelled to pray. There was nothing else left to do.

Strangely enough, even to his own surprise, he had an experience, a vision, where the cell was lit with the presence of a divine being. I had met so many people who had all sorts of experiences during my years of passionate search for God. I did not accept it or deny it, but became more attentive and asked him what was the result of it?

He explained that he was made to sew uniforms in prison, and that he rebelled against it. He would break the needles, and express his frustration in swearing. He was continually looking at the clock. But after this experience, he said he gave his heart to sewing the uniform and was surprised that he never looked at the clock. He felt so at peace while sewing or ironing the uniform. Whatever he was doing, he was with it. All sense of misery, frustration, and rebellion had disappeared. It was a transformation. The prison authorities noticed this and eventually released him. He wrote a book—*Love Can Open Prison Doors*.[14]

He would go to prisons and talk to the prisoners about the power of love and peace within, which was very satisfying and meaningful to him. Obviously, having been in prison so many times himself, he knew what it felt like—what moods, depression, anger, and rejection do to a person subject to confinement.

I met him a number of times after that. He was a caring person, tall and stately. I had always felt terrible about the logic behind the practice of punishing people for their misdeeds. The injustice of correcting wrong with wrong made little sense to me.

How could the human mind invent the electric chair? It is as great a horror as dropping the atomic bomb on civilian people. One is small, the other is big; but the cruelty is the same. At what point does justice become revenge? How can a society call itself civilized where there are wrong principles and motives in charge? You wonder if those who put other people in prison are not just as deserving, for mistreating others, because the cruelty is the same.

The unwillingness to explore the potentials of compassion for correction and healing is a cry for help itself. You wonder how many innocent and sensitive people have been incarcerated. Why would Jesus still be flogged after Pontius Pilate said, "I find no fault in this man."?[15] What is done about somebody putting a crown of thorns on his head? Where is justice within the system of justice?

Dostoyevsky, Gandhi, and Nehru, the greatest humanistic spirits, were tucked away in jails for years. The brute power of those in authority has abused geniuses throughout the ages and in all countries. If there is goodness in the world, it comes from the life of one man to the other. Who has the right to waste human life? How can we be indifferent when Life is One and minds are joined?

Let us explore the potential of goodness and rightness in relationship between man and man, open a different dimension, step out of the brutality of the past, and in our own countries, be an instrument of transformation.

How much better it would be if the world's prisons were transformed and made self-reliant. Each prison could acquire hundreds of acres of land for farming, to produce twice as much food as needed for the prison and sell the rest to support other projects. Eventually all projects could be self-reliant. Every prison could be a school to train people with skills that awaken new capacities. When they leave the prison, they would have a productive career.

We could revolutionize the prisons. It is a transformation of energy, a redirection. And it wouldn't take much. Eventually there would be hardly any expense because the prison would be productive. It is my experience that where there is goodness, there is never a lack of funds, because one is not isolated from beneficent forces at work.

There is enough goodwill in this country. Industry, corporations, foundations, universities, and individuals could participate in making the prisons and prisoners self-reliant. The resources of goodness are there for us to realize. Each person is in a prison if he limits himself to his own vested interests. These suggestions are just a beginning. We need to explore ways in which goodness could work. Exploring the potentials of caring could revolutionize our thinking.

SELFLESSNESS CAN NEVER FAIL

We have specified
the principles of the Joseph Plan—
what it is and what its resources are—
so that those students of *A Course in Miracles* who
want to be part of it
can rise to meet it.

What a boon it is for our own evolvement and growth. For the Joseph Plan introduces the eternal good within us who are blessed to give to those in need. We will be purified as we realize the potential of meriting it.

*My only function
is the one God gave me.* [16]

The Joseph Plan offers each one eternal life. What a benediction to our somewhat lost and meaningless existence. What a tragedy it would be not to see what is offered to the students of *A Course in Miracles*. In valuing the holiness of the Joseph Plan, we will recognize our own Divine function.

The life of service offers us the possibility to live by holy relationship in a distracted world that knows not what to do. It is an invitation to step out of meaningless existence and walk with God.

If we are not inspired by gratefulness, the Holy Spirit would have us read our daily Lesson once again. For the life of service offers the sanity of a living gratefulness.

It is not you who is asked to give of yourself. On the contrary, it is to you awareness is given of Grace at work in your life. For you are the Holy Son of God.

Once we realize the right perspective, we can discuss all other so-called practical and individual issues in each one's life. Removing the blocks of unwillingness to the awareness of love's presence will clear the way.

The Joseph Plan provides a life in which we are no longer caught in a situation, but freed from its bind, as well as from the littleness we impose upon ourselves.

"Love ye one another," [17] has unlimited resources. Service enriches our lives as we give ourselves to:

I give my life to God to guide today. [18]

The Joseph Plan relates the student to the sacredness of his God-created Self. How holy are you, the Holy Son of God.

I am here only to be truly helpful.
I am here to represent Him Who sent me.
I do not have to worry about what to say or what
to do, because He Who sent me will direct me.
I am content to be wherever He wishes, knowing
He goes there with me.
I will be healed as I let Him teach me to heal. [19]

Let the Christ in you listen—

> *Only God's plan for salvation
> will work.* [20]

There are so many *A Course in Miracles* students who are lost and need direction because they do not know where to begin.

BEGIN WITH HAVING TO GIVE OF YOURSELF,

says the Holy Spirit. Would you heed?

We at the Foundation ask for nothing. There is no exchange of money in it. We are merely bringing to your attention the awareness of oneness at work in your life of which you are a part. For it is you who are to bring the Kingdom of God to earth.

Unless you, yourself, see the value and the truth of this, it will not work. The Joseph Plan is an Impersonal action.

A Course in Miracles has its own independent action, a Divine action with its own force, intelligence, and vitality —a power independent of the externals. It has its own resources and Divine Intelligence. The action that brought it arranged its publishing and continued with the dissemination of almost 900,000 copies with little or no formal advertising and promotion, nor the cooperation of conve   nal large publishers.

      tive level, the action of *A Course in Miracles*
                 extend itself. The purpose of the Founda-

tion for Life Action and the Joseph Plan is to be related to and aligned with this same action that brought *A Course in Miracles* into being.

At the Foundation we started with meager means but with the resources within from the very outset. It is this self-dependence that introduced us to the Strength of Rightness. We can say with conviction that SELFLESS-NESS CAN NEVER FAIL.

The lifestyle of selfless thoughts relates you with Eternal Laws. Your own discovery of the truth that there are no problems or lack in life makes service possible.

The times are revealing that nothing external can be depended upon. You will find your inner strength in goodness. Do not isolate yourself into helplessness.

The joy of service is given to us. Let us awaken our potentials, get past illusions, and come to the actuality of—

> "Seek ye first the Kingdom of God,
> and all these things
> shall be added unto you." [21]

What a blessing to know there is no "other." We are all one, for Life is one. The power of oneness is in every man, woman and child. It is superior to the power of institutions. Within each one there is the vision of wholeness—a light.

We must respond to another's need. The very action of pure energy would humanize our lives, and peace of mind will be our wealth. Nothing is superior to a silent moment shared in service. Be grateful, and nothing of the world will affect your peace of mind. In togetherness is the inexhaustible treasure.

We all have it to give.

IN CRISIS,
IT IS YOUR CARE FOR ANOTHER
THAT WILL BE YOUR STRENGTH.

REFERENCES

References are cited for the first edition of *A Course in Miracles*, © 1975, followed in brackets by the corresponding book, chapter, section, paragraph, sentence, and page for the second edition, © 1992, of the *Course*. For example, the citation [T-16. III. 4;1. page 335.] refers to *Text*, Chapter 16, Section III, paragraph 4, sentence 1, page 335.

FOREWORD

1. *A Course in Miracles* (ACIM), first published in 1976 by the Foundation for Inner Peace, Glen Ellen, California, is a contemporary scripture that deals with the psychological/spiritual issues which face all humanity. It consists of three volumes: *Text* (I) [T], *Workbook for Students* (II) [W], and *Manual for Teachers* (III) [M]. The *Text*, 669 pages, sets forth the concepts on which the thought system of the *Course* is based. The *Workbook for Students*, 488 pages, is designed to make possible the application of the concepts presented in the *Text* and consists of three hundred-and-sixty-five lessons, one for each day of the year. The *Manual for Teachers*, 92 pages, provides answers to some of the basic questions a student of the *Course* might ask and defines many of the terms used in the *Text*.

2. *ACIM*, III, page 444. [T-22. IV. 1;1–7. page 477.]

PART I. THE STATUS QUO

1. *ACIM*, I. page 285. [T-15. III. 3;3–5. page 307.]

Chapter One: THE FUTURE OF MANKIND

1. In 1991 the United States lost a total of nearly 450,000 factory jobs. See *Facts On File*, January 16, 1992, page 21F3.

2. Swami Vivekananda as quoted in *The Dedicated: A Biography of Nivedita* by Lizelle Reymond; John Day Company, 1953, page 43. Vivekananda (1863–1902) was the direct disciple of Sri Ramakrishna and brought Vedanta to the West.

3. Swami Vivekananda, op. cit., page 47.

4. *ACIM*, II, pages 277–279. [W-153. 1;1–5 and 2;1–2 and 6;1–4 and 9;3 and 18;2. page 284.]

Chapter Two: COMING EVENTS CAST THEIR SHADOW

1. *Indira Gandhi: Letters to an American Friend* written to Dorothy Norman; Harcourt Brace Jovanovich, 1985, page 121.

2. Ibid.

3. As quoted in *Memoirs of Hope: Renewal and Endeavor* by Charles de Gaulle; Simon & Schuster, 1971, page 256.

4. As quoted in *The Legacy of Nehru*, edited by K. Natwar-Singh; John Day Company, 1965, page 107.

5. de Gaulle, op. cit., page 262.

6. From an article entitled, "Outlook 1992—State of the Union," *U.S. News & World Report*, Volume III, Number 27, December 30, 1991, page 38.

7. From an interview of Indira Gandhi by Peter Jennings on ABC's "Issues and Answers," approximately 1966.

8. From a poem by Rainer Maria Rilke.

Chapter Three: GOODNESS WILL BRING PEACE TO THE EARTH

1. *ACIM*, II, page 89. [W-55. 3;4. page 90.]

2. *ACIM*, I, page 503. [T-25. IX. 10;10. page 541.]

3. *ACIM*, III, page 8. [M-4. I. 1;4–6. page 9.]

4. *ACIM*, III, page 62. [M-26. 4;8. page 65.]

5. An excerpt from a prayer in *A Course in Miracles*, I, page 326. [T-16. VII. 12;1–7. page 350.] *Forgive us our illusions, Father, and help us to accept our true relationship with You, in which there are no illusions, and where none can ever enter. Our holiness is Yours. What can there be in us that needs forgiveness when Yours is perfect? The sleep of forgetfulness is only the unwillingness to remember Your Forgiveness and Your Love. Let us not wander into temptation, for the temptation of the Son of God is not Your Will. And let us receive only what You have given, and accept but this into the minds which You created and which You love. Amen.* This prayer has been referred to as *A Course in Miracles*' version of the Lord's Prayer. See: *Journey Without Distance: The Story Behind a Course in Miracles* by Robert

Skutch; Celestial Arts, 1984, page 68. This prayer is discussed in great detail in *Dialogues on a Course in Miracles* by Tara Singh.

6. Psalm 37:11.
7. *ACIM*, II, page 177. [W-100. page 180.]
8. *ACIM*, II, page 239. [W-133. page 245.]
9. Matthew 6:33.
10. *ACIM*, II, page 25. [W-15. page 25.]
11. *ACIM*, II, page 454. [W-325. page 464.]
12. *ACIM*, II, page 107. [W-65. page 108.]
13. *ACIM*, I, page 7. [T-1. III. 5;4. page 10.]
14. *ACIM*, II, page 450. [W-320. 2;1–3. page 460.]

Chapter Four: "I AM UNDER NO LAWS BUT GOD'S."

1. *ACIM*, I, page 326. [T-16. VII. 12;4. page 350.]
2. *ACIM*, I, introduction. [T-introduction. 2;2–3. page 1.] *Nothing real can be threatened. Nothing unreal exists.* appears in the Introduction of the *Text* of *A Course in Miracles*. The complete Introduction reads:

This is a course in miracles. It is a required course. Only the time you take it is voluntary. Free will does not mean that you can establish the curriculum. It means only that you can elect what you want to take at a given time. The course does not aim at teaching the meaning of love, for that is beyond what can be taught. It does aim, however, at removing the blocks to the awareness of love's presence, which is your natural inheritance. The opposite of love is fear, but what is all-encompassing can have no opposite. This course can therefore be summed up very simply in this way:

Nothing real can be threatened.

Nothing unreal exists.

Herein lies the peace of God.

3. *ACIM*, II, page 89. [W-55. 3;4. page 90.]
4. *ACIM*, II, page 77. [W-48. 1;1–5, page 77.]

PART II: THE AWAKENING

1. *ACIM*, I, page 54. [T-4. III. 1;12–13. page 60.]
2. *ACIM*, II, page 126. [W-73. 6;4. page 128.]

Chapter Five: THE HUMAN CRISIS—THE GAP IS INCREASING

1. The one commandment given by Jesus, "Love ye one another," appears many times in the New Testament. See, for example: John 13:34–35, 15:12, 15:17 and Romans 13:8.
2. *ACIM*, II, page 23. [W-14. page 23.]
3. Refers to the Lord's Prayer from the Sermon on the Mount. See Matthew 6:10.

Chapter Six: AMERICA'S DESTINY—Humanism

1. Swami Rama Tirtha was an Indian professor and mathematician who visited the United States in the early part of this century. For a discussion of Swami Rama Tirtha's influence on his life, see Tara Singh's *Awakening a Child from Within*; Life Action Press, 1990, pages 288–291. (Editor)
2. *Diet for a New America* by John Robbins; Stillpoint Publishing, 1987, pages 33 and 316.
3. Ibid., pages 326, 329, and 326 respectively.

Chapter Seven: AFFLUENCE WITHOUT WISDOM IS SELF-DESTRUCTIVE

1. *Love: A Fruit Always in Season—Daily Meditations* by Mother Teresa; Ignatius Press, 1987, page 228.

PART III: THE CHALLENGE

1. *ACIM*, I, page 452. [T-23. I. 1:1–5. page 486.]

Chapter Eight: WHY HAS THERE ALWAYS BEEN WAR IN THE WORLD?

1. *ACIM*, II, page 185. [W-105. 4;1–5 and 5;1–6. page 188.]
2. Matthew 5:44 and Luke 6:27.
3. John 3:6.
4. Matthew 6:10.

Chapter Nine: THE NEW AGE

1. Ancient Greek commandment written on the temple of Apollo in Delphi.

Chapter Ten: DARK FORCES

1. *ACIM*, II, page 159. [W-93. 1;1–3 and 3;1–4. page 161.]
2. *ACIM*, II, page 103. [W-62. 1;1–3. page 104.]
3. *ACIM*, II, page 101. [W-61. page 102.]
4. *ACIM*, II, page 105. [W-64. 1;2–4. page 106.]
5. *ACIM*, II, page 125. [W-73. 5;1–4. page 127.]
6. *ACIM*, II, page 101. [W-61. 1;1–6 and 2;4 and 3;2. page 102.]
7. *ACIM*, II, page 125. [W-73. 1;1–3 and 4;6. page 127.]
8. *ACIM*, II, page 162. [W-94. 2;1–6. page 164.]
9. *ACIM*, II, page 157. [W-92. 3;1–3 and 4;6–7. page 159.]
10. *ACIM*, II, page 158. [W-92, 8;1–2. page 160.]
11. *ACIM*, II, page 159. [W-93. 6;1–7. pages 161–162.]
12. *ACIM*, III, page 82. [M-Clarification of Terms. 5. 8;1–3. page 86.]

Chapter Eleven: THE FORCES THAT SWAY HUMANITY

1. Refers to: "The peace of God, which passeth all understanding." See Philippians 4:7.
2. *Commentaries on Living: Third Series* by J. Krishnamurti; The Theosophical Publishing House, 1960, page 97.
3. Refers to ". . . whosoever shall smite thee on thy right cheek, turn to him the other also." See Matthew 5:39.

Chapter Twelve: THE STILL MIND IS NOT SWAYED

1. *ACIM*, II, introduction. [T-introduction. 2;2–3. page 1.]
2. As quoted by Plato in Crito (49d), translated by Hugh Tredennick, *The Collected Dialogues of Plato*; Princeton University Press, 1961, pages 34–35.
3. Luke 9:60.

PART IV. A CALL TO SERVICE

1. *ACIM*, I, page 109. [T-7. III. 5;6–8. page 117.]

Chapter Thirteen: THE HEART OF LOVE

1. *The Life of Vivekananda and the Universal Gospel* by Romain Rolland; Advaita Ashrama, Calcutta, 1984, Backcover.

2. *Swami Vivekananda in the West: New Discoveries* (Third Edition) by Marie Louise Borke; Advaita Ashrama, Calcutta, 1983, pages 487–488.

3. *India's Walking Saint* by Hallam Tennyson; Doubleday & Co., New York, 1955, page 25.

4. Ibid., page 93.

5. *Down to Earth* by Patricia Kerr; Random House, London, 1992.

6. Story by Sue Dobson, editor and author, appeared in August 1992 issue of *Woman and Home Magazine*, London.

7. *ACIM*, III, page 1. [M-Introduction. 1;5. page 1.]

8. *ACIM*, III, page 5. [M-2. 5;5. page 6.]

9. The One Year Non-Commercialized Retreat: A Serious Study of *A Course in Miracles* took place in Los Angeles, California, from Easter, April 3, 1983 to Easter, April 22, 1984 with 50 participants from all over the United States.

10. See Genesis 37 and following.

11. May 22, 1989 issue.

12. *Samadhi*—The superconscious state in which man experiences his identity with the Ultimate Reality. (*A Brief Definition of Hinduism*, Vedanta Press, Los Angeles, CA, 1992.)

13. *ACIM*, II, page 248. [W-135. 22;2. page 255.]

14. John 15:16.

15. John 19:28.

16. Luke 2:49.

17. *ACIM*, I, Introduction. [T-Introduction. 1;7. page 1.]

18. *ACIM*, III, pages 61–62. [M-26. 1;1–3 and 4;8. pages 64–65.]

19. *ACIM*, II, page 53. [W-35. page 53.]

20. *ACIM*, I, page 98. [T-6. V-A. page 104.]

21. *ACIM*, I, page 503. [T-25. IX. 10;10. page 541.]

22. *ACIM*, I, pages 97–98. [T-6. V-A. 5;10–13 and 6;1–9. pages 105–106.]

Chapter Fourteen: THE JOSEPH PLAN

1. *ACIM*, I, page 99. [T-6. V-A. page 104.]

2. *ACIM*, I, page 1. [T-1. I. 8. page 3.]

3. *ACIM*, I, page 349. [T-18. I. 9;2. page 374.]

4. Refers to a speech Secretary of State George Marshall made June 5, 1947 at Harvard University.

5. *The Presidents Speak: The Inaugural Addresses of the American Presidents from Washington to Kennedy*; Holt, Rinehart & Winston, © 1961, page 254.

6. *Dictionary of American History*, Revised Edition. Volume V; Scribner's, © 1976, page 335.

7. *Harry S. Truman, A Biography* by Leroy Hayman; Cowell, © 1969, page 155.

8. *Plain Speaking; An Oral Biography of Harry S. Truman* by Merle Miller; Berkeley Publishing, © 1973, page 233.

9. *Dictionary of American History*, Revised Edition, Volume III; Scribner's, © 1976, page 62.

10. *ACIM*, II, page 141. [W-80. page 143.]

11. *ACIM*, I, page 405. [T-20, V. 3;6. page 435.]

12. *ACIM*, I, page 24. [T-2. V. 18;2. page 28.]

13. *ACIM*, I, page 503. [T-25. IX. 10;10. page 541.]

14. *Love Can Open Prison Doors* by Starr Daily; Arthur James, Ltd—The Drift—Evesham, Worchestershire, England, 1947.

15. New Testament, Luke 23;4.

16. *ACIM*, II, Lesson 65. [W-65. page 108.]

17. John 13:34–35 and 15:12 and 15:17.

18. *ACIM*, II, Lesson 233. [W-233. page 409.]

19. *ACIM*, I, page 24. [T-2. V. 18;2–6. page 28.]

20. *ACIM*, II, page 120. [W-71. page 121.]

21. Matthew 6:33.

OTHER MATERIALS BY TARA SINGH
RELATED TO *A COURSE IN MIRACLES*

BOOKS

Moments Outside of Time
Awakening a Child from Within
Commentaries on A Course in Miracles
How to Learn from A Course in Miracles
A Gift for All Mankind
Dialogues on A Course in Miracles
How to Raise a Child of God
"Love Holds No Grievances"—The Ending of Attack
"Nothing Real Can Be Threatened"—Exploring a Course in Miracles
Remembering God in Everything You See
Jesus and the Blind Man—A Commentary on St. John, Chapter IX
The Present Heals

AUDIO CASSETTES

Bringing A Course in Miracles into Application
Service—Finding Something of Your Own to Give
Keep the Bowl Empty
Awakening the Light of the Mind
True Meditation—A Practical Approach
In God We Trust
Conflict Ends with Me
What Is A Course in Miracles?
A Course in Miracles Explorations
"What Is the Christ?"
"Creation's Gentleness Is All I See"
Undoing Self-Deception
All Relationships Must End in Love
Is It Possible to Rest the Brain?
Discovering Your Life's Work
The Heart of Forgiveness

AUDIO CASSETTE COLLECTIONS

The Foundation for Life Action makes it possible for individuals to access the wisdom from the sharings given by Tara Singh over the ten years with his students. The following audiotape series provide a profound experience for the serious student, whether or not he/she is studying A Course in Miracles.

THE ONE YEAR NON-COMMERCIALIZED
RETREAT: A SERIOUS STUDY OF A COURSE IN MIRACLES

Seventy-two ninety-minute audiocassette tapes covering the most essential talks given by Mr. Singh during the One Year Non-Commercialized Retreat: A Serious Study of *A Course in Miracles.* Includes sharings on the *Text* and Lessons of the *Course,* Creation, Yoga, Holy Beings, Silence, Integrity, Forgiveness, and many many other topics.

HOLDING HANDS WITH YOU—
EXPLORING THE DAILY LESSON OF THE COURSE

This new twenty-five-tape series is made exclusively from Tara Singh's sharings on *A Course in Miracles Workbook* Lessons 1 to 50. Tara Singh shares profound insight, introducing the listener to key steps that will enable him or her to make his own discoveries about the lessons. They can shed a new light that brings you to the state of being that the lesson was intended to impart.

MANUAL FOR TEACHERS

This ten-tape collection is a must for dedicated students of *A Course in Miracles.* Mr. Singh brings clarity to this very important volume of the *Course* through his insightful wisdom and tremendous background.

A CALL TO WISDOM—FIVE MINUTE MEDITATIONS

Ten tapes containing seventy short messages about dealing with impurities, ending judgment, friendship, relationship, the need for certainty, productivity, intrinsic work, and the life of service, among other topics. Each message is five to ten minutes long—just enough to make space inside for a deeper contact with the truth in you.

AFTER A YEAR OF SILENCE—
SHARING THE WISDOM OF THE IMPERSONAL

This twenty-two-tape collection comes from one of the most exceptional retreats ever offered by Tara Singh. He shared the gifts of wisdom from his year of silence and laid the foundation for the Point Four Program in America by introducing the participants to what is entailed in a life of Service.

SEVEN HOLY BEINGS

A unique seven-tape set that integrates and embodies the teachings of some of the eternal beings that have deeply affected Tara Singh's life including: Jesus & The Trial, Lord Buddha, Guru Nanak, Sri Sarada Devi—the Holy Mother, Swami Vivekananda, and Saraswati—the Goddess of Music.

VIDEO CASSETTES

A Course in Miracles Is Not to Be Learned, But to Be Lived
How to Raise a Child of God
The Power of Attention
"There Must Be Another Way"
Transforming Your Life with A Course in Miracles

A free book and tape catalogue
is available upon request from:
LIFE ACTION PRESS
P.O. Box 48932
Los Angeles, California 90048
800/367-2246
213/964-5444

RETREATS AND WORKSHOPS

ANNUAL EASTER RETREAT
WITH TARA SINGH

Once each year Tara Singh meets for a week-long retreat with those of serious intent to share his wisdom on A Course in Miracles. *The location and date vary from year to year.*

To attend the retreat write or call the Foundation for Life Action at 213/933-5591 for registration information.

NATIONWIDE RETREATS
WITH STUDENTS OF TARA SINGH

Join veteran speakers, who have given their lives to living A Course in Miracles, *for a weekend retreat of exploration. Bring your questions about the* Course *or your life to students who are studying with Tara Singh. You will also explore healing relationships, discovering your Life's purpose, having something to give to another, keys to stepping out of pressure, and deepening your inner growth. Call the Foundation for Life Action at 213/933-5591 for information on retreats in your area.*

Photo courtesy of José Montenegro

ABOUT THE AUTHOR

TARA SINGH is known as a teacher, author, poet, and human-itarian. The early years of his life were spent in a small village in Punjab, India. From this sheltered environment, at the age of nine, he and his mother traveled to Panama via Europe to join his father who was in business there. While in Panama he at-tended school for two years. At the age of eighteen, he returned to India. At twenty-two, inspired by the family saint, his search for Truth led him to the Himalayas where he lived for four years as an ascetic. During this period he outgrew conventional reli-gion. He discovered that a mind conditioned by religious or secular beliefs is always limited.

In his next phase of growth, he responded to the poverty of India through participation in that country's postwar industrialization and international affairs. He became an associate of Mahatma Gandhi, and a close friend not only of Prime Minister Nehru, but also of Eleanor Roosevelt.

It was in the 1950s, as he outgrew his involvement with political and economic systems, that Mr. Singh was inspired by his association with Mr. J. Krishnamurti and the teachings of the Dalai Lama. He discovered that humanity's problems cannot be solved externally. Subsequently, he became more and more removed from worldly affairs and devoted several years of his life to the study and practice of yoga. The discipline imparted through yoga helped make possible a three-year period of silent retreat in Carmel, California, in the early 1970s.

As he emerged from the years of silence in 1976, he came into contact with *A Course in Miracles*. Its impact on him was profound. He recognized its unique contribution as a scripture and saw it as the answer to man's urgent need for direct contact with Truth. There followed a close relationship with its Scribe. The *Course* has been the focal point of his life ever since. Mr. Singh recognizes and presents the *Course* as the Thoughts of God, and correlates it with the great spiritual teachings and religions of the world.

From Easter 1983 to Easter 1984, Mr. Singh conducted the One Year Non-Commercialized Retreat: A Serious Study of *A Course in Miracles*. It was an unprecedented, in-depth exploration of the *Course*. No tuition was charged. Since then, Mr. Singh has worked on a one-to-one basis with a small group of serious students under the sponsorship of the Foundation for Life Action.